D1808603

Front Cover Ilustration: Grape Day in Escondido
on Grand Ave. looking east in 1914.

Panorama: A view of Escondido looking east from Howell Heights in 1897.

Escondido History
&
★ *The Grape Day Celebration* ★

By
Douglas Westfall

The Paragon Agency, Publishers
Orange, CA
2005

Escondido History
&
The Grape Day Celebration

Douglas Westfall 1949—

Published by
The Paragon Agency
Orange, California
2005

1. Escondido
2. California Farmlands
3. California History
   I. Title
   II. Author

Library of Congress Control Number: 2004098848

ISBN: 1-891030-39-6

©2005 The Paragon Agency
All Rights Reserved

No part of this book may be reproduced
without the previous written consent
of the publisher.

Printed in the USA
1k, r1

DEDICATION

This book is dedicated to Escondido's residents,
past, present, and future.

PREFACE

The publisher wishes to thank the many historic photographers, who contributed greatly to this publication. One of whom was Louis Havens, here shown with his 8 x 10 view camera at the northwest corner of 2nd Avenue and Hickory Street.

Louis Havens

FOREWORD

Escondido is a special place. Whether you grew up here, recently moved to Escondido, or are just passing through, I think you'll find the history of our community interesting. Local history grounds us. It gives us roots in the fast paced, global world we live in today. This book, which examines the valley's long heritage, also emphasizes Escondido's unique Grape Day, and illustrates what sets us apart from anyplace else.

I hope that after reading this book, you will be inspired to learn even more about our community. Since 1956, we have collected and preserved Escondido's history. Tour our museum in Grape Day Park, visit our website, or attend the revived Grape Day Festival in September. You'll see even more of the great photographs in our collection and gain a deeper appreciation for this beautiful hidden valley.

Wendy Barker
Director
Escondido History Center

CONTENTS

x

Chapter 1
NATIVE ESCONDIDO

*"Wherever there were oak trees
and water ... Indians lived."*
Leo Calac, Native American

Escondido lies in a valley, behind three peaks of moderate height, between the mountains and the sea. Traveling from the ocean, the small mountain chain appears to blend with the Santa Rosa mountains to the east, keeping the valley from easily being seen.

The source for the name of the city of Escondido is lost to time, although early Spanish references to the name Escondido, always referred to hidden water — a greatly desired resource in the arid countryside of Southern California. Juan Bautista de Anza opened the route to California from Sonora, Mexico in 1774 and repeated the journey in 1775-76 with a large party of colonists. He named two water sites as Escondido, but neither are anywhere near the Escondido of today, and Anza's nearest approach to the valley was more than fifty miles away.

Rancho Rincon del Diablo was the first recorded name on the land, but the creek was named Escondido. By the early 1880s, a Post Office called Apex was near the northern point of the old rancho boundary. Within three years it was moved and renamed Escondido after the creek. Later the man-made lake had the name as well, until it was changed to Lake Wohlford in the 1924. The reservoir created constant flow in Escondido Creek and since that time, it has been known as both creek and river. There are two other Escondido creeks in California.

The area's recorded history essentially dates to the Mexican period of California, yet early Native Americans left their mark in the form of petroglyphs several thousand years ago. The carvings left in stone are found throughout the region and the state, yet are rare enough to require preservation.

Little else of these early people's culture remained however, after their descendants were later absorbed into the Spanish Mission system. During the Mexican period, the Missions were

Local Indian pictographs

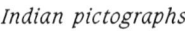

Indian pictographs

Mission Indian Chapel.

The church at Pala.

dissolved and Indian towns were established. These too were suspended during the early American era.

The Native Americans of the immediate region, are referred to as the *Luíseño* and today, identify themselves as *Puyumkowitchum,* or Western People. South of today's Escondido are the *Kumeyaay* or *Digueño* tribe. Originally, the Luíseño lived near the water and food sources of the area. They resided in willow framed homes, covered with brush, tulles or tree branches.

The Spanish arrival in California in 1769 brought the Mission system and development of ranching and agriculture, using the Native Americans as a labor pool. Other than the

San Luis Rey Mission – 1892.

absorption of the local Native American culture, Spanish intrusion into this area was limited to agricultural fields and a few Indian Chapels. Mission San Luís Rey, founded in 1795, incorporated the Indians of this area, giving them the name Luíseño after the mission. Essentially, the Missions then controlled all the lands, and for all the development of missions, presidios and pueblos, the Spanish were here but 52 years.

The transfer to the Mexican government in 1822 brought

Three Indian women at San Luis Rey – 1900.

little change for a dozen years, then the mission lands were given away into some 800 ranchos, throughout the territory. The Mexican government ruled only 25 years, when the Mexican American war brought California into the United States in 1847.

Active development of the countryside did not occur until 20 years after the 1850 statehood, with the final dissolution of the local ranchos. Slightly over 600 of the original ranchos were approved by a land commission and those remaining quickly changed into American hands.

The town of Escondido was established on one of these ranchos, but not for 30 years after it was first sold to an American. The original 12,814 acres of the town remained until the 1950s, when annexation began. The city today is well beyond ten times the size of that original town.

The real story of Escondido begins 90 million years ago, when a giant batholith of molten rock, began an uplift of the peninsular ranges, creating the valley between the two granite chains. Intrusions of other molten rock, brought the mineralization of gold, silver, copper, nickel and tungsten, for which the region is justly famous. Created with the uplift of the peninsular ranges, were the three peaks: Mt. Whitney, Double Peak, and Frank's Peak.

The Escondido valley is a triangular shaped basin held up by a volcanic rock base, formed during the Cretaceous period (65-135 million years ago.) No evidence of dinosaurs roaming here exists, as the land went under a period of immense erosion, greatly altering the landscape. A creek intermittently flowed from the mountains through the valley, and then to the sea.

A significant gold district was discovered in American times and centered around what is now Julian, up in the high country of the Cleveland National Forest. Julian became a major gold producing region, with hundreds of mines operating in the 1850s. Escondido too, had its share of gold mines, starting up in American times.

The area however, is more renowned today for the gemstones found in the 25-mile-long belt which yields treasures like tourmaline, spodumene, beryl, topaz and garnet. The Gemological Institute of America deservedly, is located near the shore in northern San Diego county, west of Escondido.

Dozens of gem mines exist today, within easy driving range of the city. Three primary gemstone districts are Pala, Rincon, and Mesa Grande, and over the years, these have provided millions of dollars in gems. But Pala, Rincon and Mesa Grande regions have another important qualities: they

Beryl, one of the many semi-precious stones found in the vicinity of Escondido.

are centers of Native American populations.

For thousands of years, the Native Americans lived in the valley of Escondido. The plentiful oak groves and available water attracted small groups of Indians, living near the canyons and waterways. Their homes were built from a circle of willow boughs that were curved and tied together with yucca cord at the center. Stones were set at the base of the poles, around the home. To repel the rain, they were covered with brush, or tulles when available.

Native metates (mortars) and manos (hand pestles) have been found in several areas and the site of a village was discovered in 1913, at the east end of the Eureka Ranch in Escondido.

A variety of plants from yucca to acorn meal, supplied the staples of these early peoples diet. The milling holes at former village sites attest to the use of grinding acorns, and a type of local grain was cultivated near the coast and this was traded to

Metates

the people of the hills and the mountains. Wetlands near the coast provided celery, lettuce and watercress. Ocean fish and shellfish were also traded as was salt, tar and sea shells.

Small animals were hunted with bow and arrow, made from willow with dear sinew and willow shafts with stone and even wooden arrowheads. Coastal antelope and woodland deer were the primary large animals that were hunted. Bows and arrows were also the primary means of defense.

Indian ramadas were constructed of willow frames with brush used to create shade. Pottery was fired in open pits for dinner ware and larger vessels were used for storing food. Baskets were created from juncus, sumac and muhlenbergia reeds and grasses; clothing was made from the same materials.

When the natives moved away, or the homes got too old, or if their homes became infested with insects, the houses were simply burned. Reconstruction was simple and sufficient to endure another year.

Today the Luíseño have established their sovereign rights as independent Native Americans and are located at the Rincon,

Indian Woman

Pauma, and La Jolla Reservations. In 1988 the Indian Gaming Regulatory Act opened up tribal gaming, and two years later, Congress exacted the Native American Grave Protection and

Repatriation Act. Twelve bands collaborated within San Diego county in 1997, and four years later, casinos opened at Campo, Pala, Pauma, Rincon and the San Pasqual Reservations.

Although Native Americans have been in the Escondido area for thousands of years, recorded history within the valley essentially began in 1845 during the end of the Mexican era. Three ranchos were established in the immediate area and one, at the present center of the city of Escondido.

Native American women gathering and grinding pine nuts and acorns.

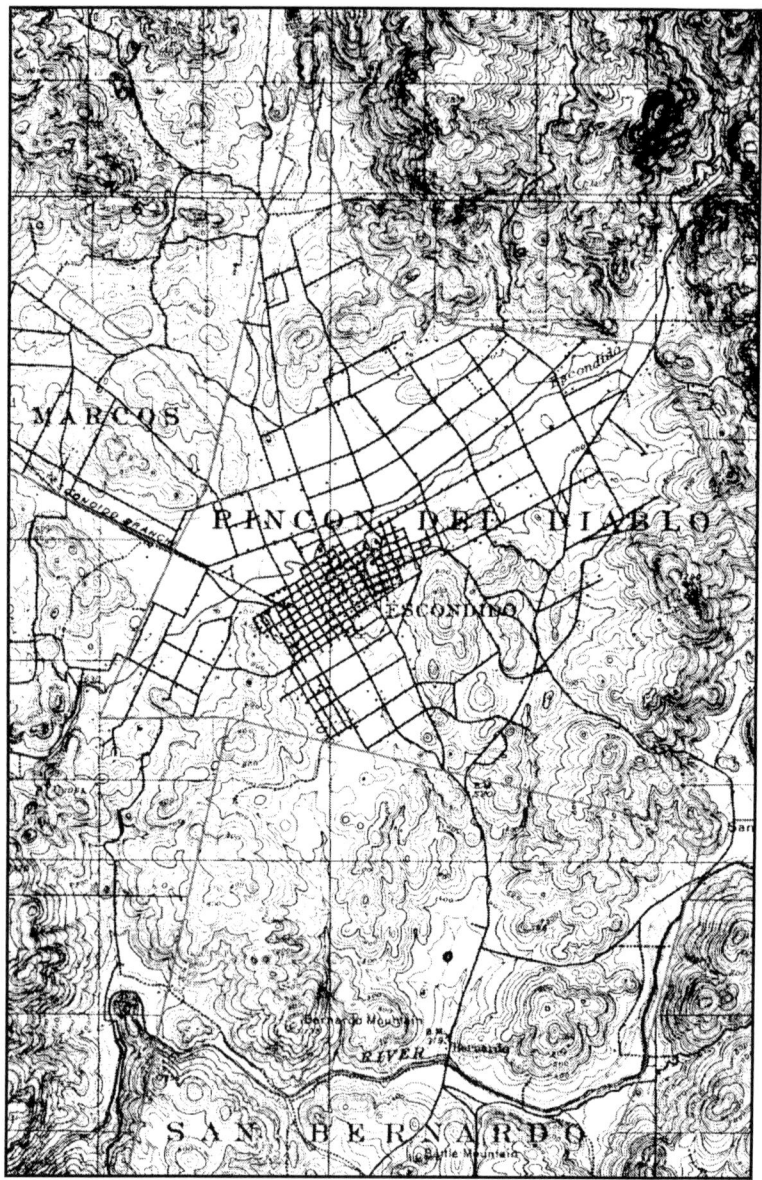

Early map of Escondido showing the original Rancho boundaries.

Chapter 2
HISPANIC RANCHOS

*"We marched toward San Diego in the
direction of San Bernardo...it was deserted except
by a few Indians."*
Lt. William Emory

Located about fifteen miles from the ocean, Juan Bautista Alvarado established the Rancho *Rincón del Diablo* in 1843. His birth in Santa Barbara during 1790 was little more than a blessed event: he had 14 brothers and sisters. Their parents were from Presidio Loreto in Baja California, and came to Alta California in 1789. All the children were born in California except their oldest sister, born at Loreto.

The Spanish missions had vast land holdings — up to nine leagues radiating out from the mission site. These were to be dispersed after fifteen years, to the Native Americans who had built up the ranches and farms. The Padres however, felt the Indians had not attained the ability to care for such large and valuable lands and so continued to have the church maintain their holdings. In half a century of Spanish presence in California, no mission was ever secularized.

The Indians in New Spain revolted in 1810, as did eventually all indigenous people throughout Latin America, and in 1821 the free Republic of Mexico was established. It was a year before the new Mexican government came to California to take over the Presidios and the office in Monterey, but by the end of 1822 little had changed.

The Spanish had left 19 missions, 4 presidios, 3 pueblos and a scattered collection of asistencias, estancias and Indian capillas (chapels.) Perhaps no more than 30 Spanish ranchos were remaining in existence; there had never been more than 40. These were concessions *(Concedos)* not grants. Several Rancheros had even made requests to partition and even sell·off their ranchos. This was illegal under Spanish law and remained so under the new Mexican regime.

At the time, there were no ranchos in what is now San Diego county. The presidio and mission at San Diego, plus the mission at San Luís Rey were the primary holdings. Several Indian chapels were scattered inland, and the two asistencias: San Pedro de Las Flores on the coast and the inland San Antonio de Pala,

Front view of the Mission San Diego.

were about all there was. Indian chapels at Cahuilla (1782), Pauma (1790), Temecula (1798), Santa Ysabel (1816), and Rincon were well established and others would follow at La Jolla, Mesa Grande, Pechanga and Santa Rosa.

Of course there were the vast land holdings of the two missions. Ten years later in 1832, the laws changed favorably concerning ranchos and their establishment. Ranchos could be divided and portions sold off. Many of the larger ranchos went through this process, usually for the children of original Ranchero.

In 1834 the missions were secularized (made public,) and the tide came in. Between then and 1846 — only a dozen years — some 800 ranchos were founded, mostly on former mission lands. There were thirty ranchos in San Diego county alone.

Native towns or Indian Pueblos, came from the secularization of the mission lands. Mission buildings were relegated to the status of churches and the Mission Indians had no place to go. Three Indian Pueblos were established in San Diego county: one at San Pascual, named for the 16th century Franciscan, Saint Paschal.

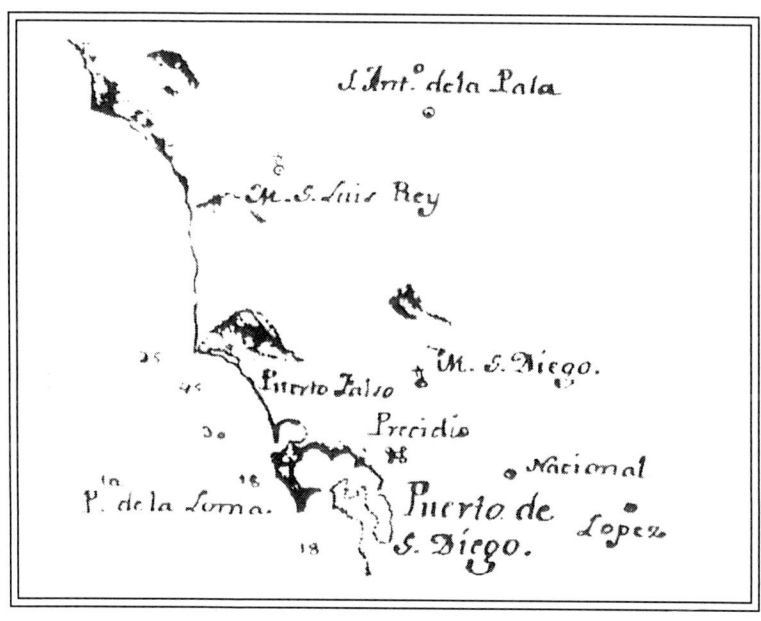

San Diego in 1830.

At San Pascual, the Native Americans were given the entire valley; Rancho San Bernardo eventually adjoined the pueblo on the western edge. There were eighty-one native people at the new town, all from the former Mission San Diego.

There were several Juan Bautista Alvarados in California at the time, presumably all related the century before. One was Juan Bautista Valentin Alvarado, the governor of California from 1836 to 1842. The year 1836 was one of turmoil in California — there were five governors in that year alone. Governor Alvarado was part of the revolution against Governor Nicolás Gutiérrez, who had attempted governorship twice that year, yet only for a total sum of less than seven months.

Governor Alvarado brought stability to California and restarted the establishment of ranchos, even permitting a rancho to be founded by a distant relative, José María Alvarado. *Rancho Los Vallecitos de San Marcos,* (35,573 acres) came in 1840 to this Alvarado. Previously the valley had been discovered by a military escort on April 25 in 1797 — the year before the founding of nearby Mission San Luís Rey. This had been St. Mark's day and the 'Little Valley of San Marcos,' was so named. As late as 1835, it was listed as a small farm, belonging to the

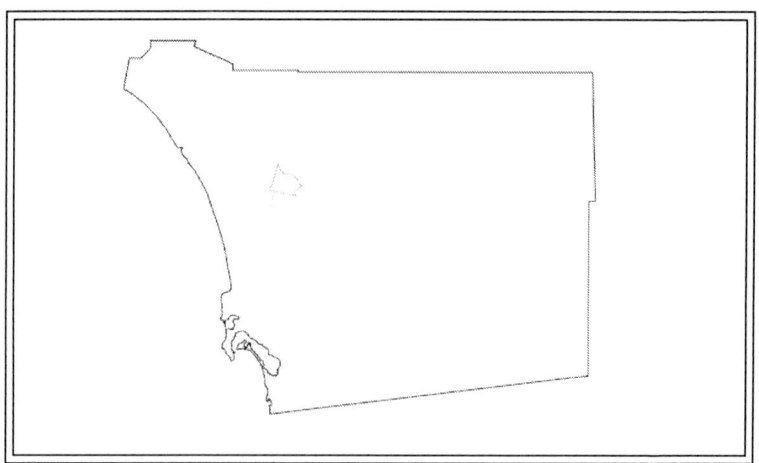

San Diego county showing the location of Rancho Rincon del Diablo.

Rancheros capturing a horse.

mission. Juan Maria Alvarado petitioned Governor Alvarado in April of 1840 and received the rancho the same year.

During this brief period of unrest in 1836, an English sea captain, Joseph Snook, had been cooperative with the new government. He had established himself as a Mexican citizen in 1833 and was familiar with the area around San Diego. Snook petitioned for a rancho in 1841 and the following year received *Rancho Arroyo de San Bernardo*. Later in 1845, Snook received additional land, bringing the rancho to 17,763 acres.

Snook's adopted name of *José Francisco de Sales* reverted to José Snook after a time when he married his neighbor's daughter, Maria Antonio Alvarado. The Rancho San Bernardo is named for the creek which was named as (the place of) *El Paraje o Canada de San Bernardo* in 1821 for Bernard of Clairvaux. Bernard, a French Saint, started the Second Crusade during the 1100s. The creek is now called the San Dieguito River, it is largely covered by Lake Hodges as is the former town of Bernardo.

The Mexican government then felt that Governor Alvarado needed replacement and sent Manuelo Micheltorena to replace him. The new governor remained in office until 1845, when he

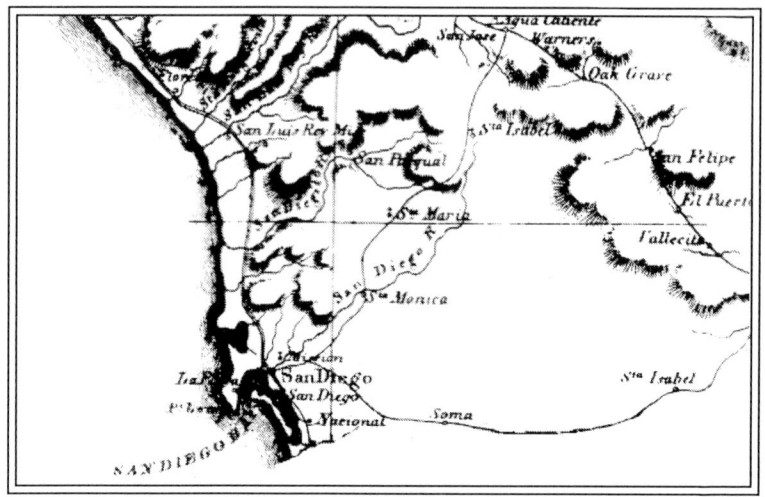

San Diego area.

was overthrown by Pio de Jesus Pico — the last Mexican Governor of California.

After the takeover by Pio Pico, Governor Pico gave out many land grants, including one to himself: Rancho Santa Marguerita Y Las Flores, a 133,441 acre property, made from two former ranchos, and now referred to as Camp Pendleton.

In late 1845, Pico awarded the Rancho *Guejito y Cañada de Palomea* to José María Orosco. East of Escondido, the Rancho Guejito was 13,299 acres in size.

Orosco also married his neighbor's daughter, Guadalupe Alvarado. *Guejito* means pebbles and *Palomea* is a type of dove. The canyon of the doves/pebbles is as close to a translation as can be had. The Guejito rancho today is still in place as a cattle ranch, it is one of the few remaining ranchos in all California.

During Governor Micheltorena's office however, he awarded the 12,654 acre *Rancho Rincón del Diablo* to Juan Bautista Alvarado — a distant relative of the Alvarado, Micheltorena had replaced in office. It was the smallest of the four ranchos. This Alvarado, now of San Diego, had married María Raymundo

Fermína Nepomucena Yorba, a daughter (one of many) of Antonío Yorba, a Catalan volunteer at Monterey in 1771. Juan and María were nineteen and sixteen respectively, and had met while he was in Los Angeles. Over time they had six children: Francisco, Juan María, Guadalupe, María Antonia, Isabella and José Maria. They lived at San Diego where he was *regidor de ayuntamiento* (on the city council) in 1835, *commissario de policia* (police commissioner) the following year, and in the *disputacíon de Alta California* (territorial assembly) three years after that. By the time Alvarado received his rancho, he was 53.

The origin of the name of the Rancho Rincón del Diablo, is lost to history. Of some 200 place names in California (in both Spanish and English) that are named for the devil, virtually all are named for geologic features. *El Camiño del Diablo* is the road in a desert, Rancho *Cañada del Diablo* is in a steep walled canyon, Rancho *Monte del Diablo,* is a mountain. For the Rancho Rincón del Diablo however, there is no known source.

Juan Alvarado built a six room adobe dwelling in the southern corner of the rancho and raised cattle. José María Alvarado (San Marcos) and Juan Bautista Alvarado (Rincón del Diablo) were definitely cousins however, their lineage to Governor Juan Bautista Valentin Alvarado had not been proven.

Alvarado raised cattle, and sold them in San Diego. Most ranchos were cattle ranches, and the hides were more valuable than the meat as the meat could not be preserved. In addition to clothing, leather was used to make beds, chairs, door hinges, and many other products because forged metal was rare. American ships traded at major ports for raw leather and brought manufactured goods back to California.

During Spanish times, trade was very restricted although many ships traded illegally along the California shore at smuggler's ports. Furs were much more valuable than hides and could bring ten times as much for the same number of items. At the time, the peso equalled a dollar, and illegal trades in San Diego county could bring $1,500 per trade — ten times the annual salary of a soldier at the presidio.

In the Mexican period however, trade was open and

Every spring, while calves were still with their mothers, the vaqueros branded the cattle to identify them from other ranchos.

smuggling decreased as high priced trades in furs dwindled. Cattle hides were the primary merchandise and the many cattle ranchos supplied the trade with a large volume of goods.

The vaquero (literally cow-boy) worked the ranch and the cattle. The European population in Spanish times was never over 1,500 people in all of California. Most of these were the families of the soldiers at the presidios and missions. As retiring soldiers began to start ranchos, cowboys were needed to operate the vast herds of cattle and the Native Americans began to leave the missions for rancho life. In California, the Indians were the cowboys — vaqueros, and literally roamed the range on horseback.

The year 1845 found the four ranchos in place — María Antonia Alvarado had married the Englishman José Snook and Guadalupe Alvarado had married José Orosco — both Juan Bautista Alvarado's daughters. His son, Juan Maria Alvarado of San Marcos married Lugarda Dionisia Osuna. The adjacent ranchos of *Los Vallecitos de San Marcos, Arroyo de San Bernardo, Rincón del Diablo* and neighboring *Guejito y Cañada de Palomea* were now neighbors of the Indian Pueblo, San Pascual. That same year, Governor Pico came into power (his second time,) and California was ripe for the picking.

An American flag was raised over Hawk's Peak (now Fremont) in the winter of 1845, yet the Mexican American war in California was not initiated until early May of 1846. Within a month, the Americans began seizing primary towns: Sonoma, Yerba Buena (San Francisco,) Monterey, Los Angeles, and San Diego. They did this primarily with US Naval ships anchored at principal ports, raising the American flag at each one. Battles ranged from Santa Clara county in the north, to San Diego county in the south.

Initially, the Americans captured Sonoma on June 14, and the battle of Olompali happened the next day. With the seizure of Monterey at the beginning of the war on July 7, the war went in the American's favor. After continuing the capture of primary cities during July and the seizure of Los Angeles in early August, California was declared under American control on August 17 of 1846.

Three battles then ensued in Los Angeles, Chino, and Dominguez where the Mexican forces won all three; this was in late September and early October. Following these battles, a cease fire was called and Mexico was thought to hold California.

General Stephen Watts Kearny had left Fort Leavenworth, Kansas during June, marching toward California. Capturing Santa Fe, New Mexico, Kearny divided his troops and with 300 men, headed west. Meeting up with scout Kit Carson, an erroneous message was relayed that California had been taken by the Americans. With this, Kearny sent 200 troops back to Santa Fe, and with only 100 men, moved on to California.

Kearny, led by Carson and accompanied by Lt. William Emory, entered California

Kit Carson

through the desert, stopping at Warner's Ranch to rest. Coming into the valley of San Pasqual, Kearny met with General Andres Pico (the governor's brother,) and the Mexican troops on December 6th. Attacking at dawn, Kearny was overwhelmed. Each side ended with a similar number of wounded, and Pico had lost but one man. Kearny however, had lost 21 men and sent Carson and a lieutenant to San Diego for reinforcements with help from an Indian guide.

General Stephen Watts Kearny

Two of Alvarado's sons were at the battle; Jose María went with several men to the Pauma Rancho for safety after the battle. They were captured by a band of Indians and killed, being one of the few Indian attacks in the history of California.

The Indians at San Pasqual however, elected to help the Americans and, it is said, an Indian girl came to the rescue of the wounded. Surrounded by the Mexican troops, and with such a loss of manpower, the Americans under Kearny had little hope. Private Dunne stated: *"An Indian from San*

General Andres Pico

Mexican American War

Pascual reached the hill." He guided Lt. Beale and Kit Carson to San Diego, allowing for the support of troops and the rescue of the Americans. The Mexicans had won the battle, but the Americans were about to win the war.

Kearny gained reinforcements and left for Los Angeles. The battle of the San Gabriel river took place on January 8th, with a captured cannon from Los Angeles, and the Americans won.

There was another American win at La Mesa on January 9th and a third win in Natividad (near Monterey,) on January 10th. Pico and the Mexican troops capitulated on January 13. California was now in American hands. From the first battle in June, to the surrender in January, 1847, the war lasted little over six months within California. In that year, the population of San Diego county was just over 2,000 people.

Some 80 years later, nearly two acres of land in the San Pasqual valley was donated to the State of California, as a remembrance to those that died in the battle.

The marker reads in part:

The State of California honors with this monument, the American soldiers who, under the leadership of Brig. Gen. Stephen W. Kearny, Capt. Abraham R. Johnson, Capt. Benjamin Lee Moore, Edward F. Beale, USN and Kit Carson the scout, gave their lives in the Battle of San Pasqual between the Americans and the Mexicans, December 6-10, 1846.

The plaque goes on to list 20 men.

The signing of the Treaty of Guadalupe Hidalgo — peace between Mexico and America — occurred on February 2nd, 1848, transferring California to the United States. When gold was discovered in Sutter's millrace, no one at Guadalupe knew of the discovery of gold, which happened nine days before the signing of the treaty.

The Battle of Pasqual in December of 1846 was the turning point for the Mexican American War in California. Within the proximity of modern Escondido, it had a decisive effect on the future of California.

Juan Bautista Alvarado was buried in the Plaza Church of Los Angeles on January 11th, 1847. The event of his death is unrecorded but took place three days after the nearby battle of the San Gabriel River.

With Alvarado's death in 1847, his daughter María Snook took over

San Pasqual marker placed in 1925.

some control of the Rancho Rincón del Diablo, but her husband died the following year. In 1853 María married again, to another Englishman: Henry Clayton. Now the Alvarado families had both ranchos to manage as America was coming into control of California. Many ranchos changed hands after the American takeover and the *Rincón del Diablo* was no different.

Ranchos in San Diego County

Grant Number	Name	Acres
505	Santa Margarita y Las Flores	133,441
506	Monserate	13,323
507	Pauma	13,310
508	Valle de San José	17,634
509	San José del Valle	26,689
510	Santa Ysabel	17,719
511	Valle de San Felipe	9,972
512	Cuyamaca	35,501
513	Cañada de San Vicente y Mesa del Padre Barrona	13,316
514	Valle de Pamo or Santa María	17,719
515	Guejito	13,299
516	Rincon del Diablo	12,654
517	Vallecitos de San Marcos	8,975
518	Buena Vista	2,288
519	Guajomé	2,219
520	Ex-Mission San Luis Rey	53
521	Agua Hedionda	13,311
522	Los Encenitos	4,431
523	San Dieguito	8,825
524	San Bernardo	17,763
525	Los Penasquitos	8,486
527	San Diego, Island of	4,185
528	La Nacíon	26,632
529	Otay (Estudillo)	6,658
530	Otay (Dominguez)	4,437
531	Jamacha	8,881
533	Mission San Diego	22.21
534	El Cajon	48,800
535	Cañada de los Coches	28.39
538	Cuca or El Potrero	2,174
541	Jamul	8,926

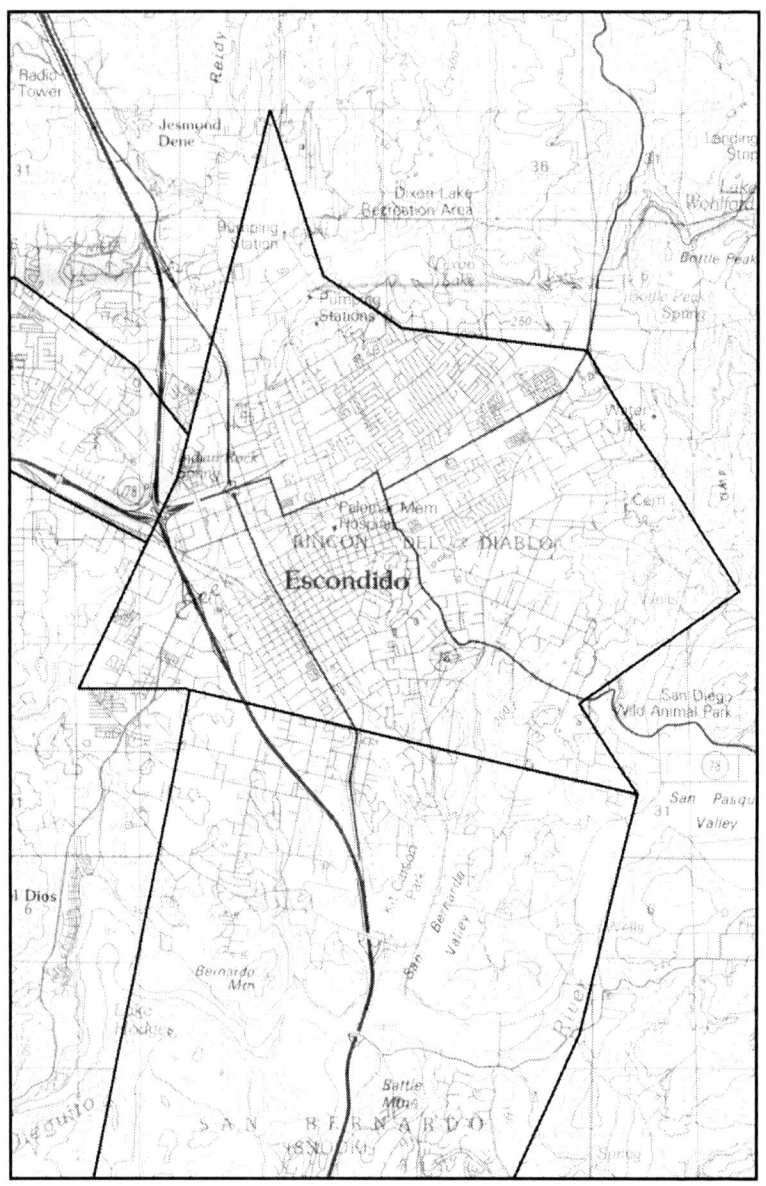

Present day map of Escondido, showing the three Rancho boundaries.

Chapter 3
AMERICAN RANCHES

*"I regard Escondido people as the salt
of the earth, as the saying goes."*
Midwesterner on moving to Escondido

Judge Oliver S. Witherby started buying the Rincón del Diablo rancho in 1855. He was a boundary commissioner in San Diego at the close of the war, in which the delegation from California and Mexico, were there to place the international boundary. The Mexican delegation had wanted San Diego to remain part of Mexico, but the Americans held out.

In the previous year of 1854, a United States Land Commission was formed to validate the many land holdings within California, and to convert the Mexican land grants into US land patents. Of some 800 land claims submitted, over 200 were rejected. Less than 100 appealed that decision, which resulted in just over 600 approved ranchos. Of those, little more than half were owned by those with a hispanic surname.

Title to Rincón del Diablo was confirmed in 1876, 21 years after it was sold. Guejito was confirmed in 1866, with San Marcos in 1869, and San Bernardo in 1874. Ranchos continued to be transferred out of Californio hands by legal and unscrupulous means.

Beginning in 1855, two daughters of Juan Bautista Alvarado sold their share of the Rincón del Diablo to Judge Witherby for

$666.66. Seemingly an odd sum, this would indicate that the whole rancho was then evaluated at $2,000, as there were six children, and their collective one third was $333.33 each. María Antonia Snooks and Guadalupe Orosco sold first, probably because they had ranchos of their own.

Judge Oliver S. Witherby

Late in that same year, Francisco and the children of Juan María (who died at Pauma,) sold for $1,000. Isabella held out for two years and received $2,050. At that time, even though he did not own the entire rancho, Witherby moved onto the property. He had a large adobe home built, adjacent to the Alvarado adobe.

Witherby never married, but focused his energy on farming and extending the ranching operations to include sheep. Cattle was still a growing business, as miners in northern California needed them for meat, and cattle drives north were common. Now cattle were desired for food, rather than leather and the ranchos still thrived. In the 1860s, Witherby began a gold mining operation which later grew to include a 5-stamp mill.

Called the *Rincón del Diablo and Escondido Mining Company,* Witherby wrote a letter in 1861 using the name of his mine, which was the first recorded use of the name Escondido in written form. The creek had been called Escondido for some time, and ran through the center of his property.

In 1862, the last surviving son of Juan Bautista Alvarado, José María, evidently gave in and sold his remaining interest in the property for only $100. In total, Judge Witherby had paid nearly

Remains of the Juan Bautista Alvarado adobe – 1892

$4,000 for well over 12,000 acres of land, over the course of seven years. That same year however, Witherby mortgaged his property for $1,000, with an interest at 18% per annum.

By late 1862, heavy rains came to southern California and between 1863 and 1864 no rain fell at all. During the greatest

Longhorn cattle on the ranchos of California.

Indian vaqueros tended the cattle.

drought in California, cattle died by the thousands. Some rancheros shot their horses, just to save the feed for the cows. In 1865 and 1866, many ranchos were lost and changed hands. The year 1867 brought floods again — the greatest flood in southern California history — but by then cattle operations had ceased all over the south land.

In 1868, Witherby sold his ranch for $8,000, twice what he had paid for it only a dozen years before. Witherby moved to San Diego and got into high finance. He lost it all in the financial crash of 1893 and died three years later.

Edward McGeary had bought half of Witherby's ranch. His partners bought the other half with one of them taking over Witherby's adobe.

These were Mathus Wolfskill and sons John and Josiah. The Wolfskill family began with William Wolfskill, a fur trapper, who came to Los Angeles in 1831. William was the first to build a schooner in California (1832) and the first to grow oranges (1841), both in the Los Angeles area. He also had a vineyard in Los Angeles in the 1830s, which was present on the land when he bought it. That vineyard started the grape industry in California.

Remains of the Judge Oliver S. Witherby adobe

Many of Wolfskill's family raised grapes as well throughout California. He too, became a Mexican citizen and married a local girl, María Magdalena de Jesus Lugo. His family and their lands were extensive throughout California; Mathus (Mathias) was his brother.

Pedro José Ponto Escarcar, a Native American, had been baptized in 1817 at the new Santa Isabel Chapel at age 14. Years later, he became the leader of the band that had settled the San Pasqual Indian Pueblo. Considered the captain of the town, it was Ponto that had led the two Americans to San Diego during the Battle of San Pasqual.

The story of Ponto, was related by his daughter Felicita.

"That afternoon Pontho, my father, called his men together and asked them if they wished to help the Americanos in their trouble. The men said they did. When darkness was near Pontho sent a messenger to the Mexican chief telling him to trouble the Americans no more that night else the Indians would help the Americans. And the Mexican chief heeded the message and the Americans were left to bury their dead and to rest because of my father's message. The Americanos do not know of this but my people know of it."

Felicita as reported in:
<u>Indian History in San Pasqual</u> by Elizabeth Judson Roberts

In 1852, Ponto was one of the chiefs who signed a peace treaty with the United States. He continued to have the US government recognize Native American rights. Ponto died in 1874 while preparing to travel to Washington DC.

After his death, the population at San Pasqual waned. By 1878, less than 200 Native Americans were living at the Indian town.

In that year, a court order came with the county deputy

Felicita La Chappa

sheriff, to remove the Native Americans from their lands. Through a legal maneuvering, an American had found a way to obtain the property. The wooden homes were burned and with only an adobe church left standing, the people went on to other Native American villages in the area.

W. Perry Bevington had claimed their lands in a San Diego County Superior Court. The representatives of the town were not allowed to speak and a Writ of Ejectment was approved, allowing the removal of the Indians. Bevington later received title to the property, much of which is now a State Park.

On the Wolfskill ranch, John first lived in the Witherby adobe on the southern edge with his wife, where Alvarado's adobe had been reduced to a few walls by the rains. He later built a wood frame house in the northern area of the ranch (North Broadway,) and became the resident manager for the partnership. McGeary resided in Los Angeles — largely as a silent partner.

This chapel was part of the Indian settlement in San Pasqual Valley.

The Wolfskills farmed grain, grew orchards, and herded cattle but soon changed over to sheep ranching. The weathered landscape allowed little else in the form of ranch operations. One of the Wolfskills removed a squatter, Pierre Renand, by paying $1 in gold coin for what Renand claimed was his. This added 160 adjacent acres to the Wolfskill property.

Sheep ranching had round-ups, just like cattle ranching, but the sheep round-ups were for shearing, not branding. Dogs were used to control the sheep and shearers were brought in at 5¢ an animal. A good shearer could make $25 a day; the best could make $50. In the 1870s, that was high wages.

The Bernardo Rancho was sold in 1867 to James McCoy of Ireland. He ran sheep like the Wolfskills, and was later elected to the California State Senate. The San Bernardo Rancho was divided and there began the town of Bernardo at Mule Hill. Zenas Sikes moved onto the Rancho Bernardo and cultivated 2,400 acres in wheat and barley in the eastern end of the valley. He eventually became Bernardo's first postmaster, but died in 1881

Wolfskill Ranch

from a kick by a horse. (Sikes' adobe is now open to the public.) Ransford Lewis later bought the property plus the area now including Felicita Park.

There was a school at Jesmond Dene and the post office, and a school at Rock Springs; all in 1881. Charles McDougall was postmaster for a year, then Thomas Adams took over and moved the post office to his house in 1883.

For 15 years the ranch, now known as the *Wolfskill Plains,* was known as a sheep ranch and had up to 12,000 sheep roaming the valley. The climate however, with available water from the Escondido Creek, allowed the cultivation of grapes and these they grew in quantity. Grapes would always be associated with Escondido.

It was the success of the ranch and the vineyards that attracted a syndicate of investors in 1883. The crossroads near Escondido Creek was called Apex (as was the postoffice,) and people were moving west where land speculation was common.

The Stockton Company from the San Joaquin valley of California, offered $10 an acre for the ranch; the Wolfskills and McGary had paid little over $1.50 — this was six times their

Town of Bernardo

investment. This amounted to more than $128,000, although much of the money came from mortgages, in all 15 were required — one for each investor. In 1883, the Wolfskills returned to the Los Angeles area, with John moving his family to Pasadena. All of them retired very wealthy.

The Stockton Company brought in grapevines; a hardy variety known as *muscat grapes*. These required little water, and the creek — the primary water source — was intermittent at best in the arid climate.

Imported from Europe, the muscat grapes grew well and the *'Big Vineyard,'* (also called the Hadopian & Setrakien Company field,) was planted adjacent to Escondido Creek, (now Rose and Washington.) What followed was an extraordinary ten month rain. That year of 1883, over 50 inches fell and ruined the grape crop. The Stockton Company began looking for a buyer.

In the following year of 1884, the Apex post office was renamed to Escondido and within that year, the Stockton Co. transferred all rights to the newly formed *Escondido Company*. They were looking to sell.

Two years followed and in 1886, a new group of investors bought the entire property for just over $100,000 — and paid off all the mortgages. They also gave $20 to Guadalupe Alvarado Orosco

Big Vineyard

The Wolfskill ranch became of the headquarters of the Escondido Land & Town Co. – c.1887

Martinez as she had remarried and still lived on part of the old rancho. Ranching was always a part of the land.

A population boom was growing in California and the new group known as the Escondido Land and Town Company (EL&TCo,) planned to create a town and sell lots for a farming community. EL&TCo was comprised of the four Thomas brothers (there were five,) plus eight other investors. Part of the group had organized the towns of Ramona and San Marcos and others were on the board of the San Diego Central Railroad Company.

The Thomas brothers ran the operation: Richard handled the financial operations, William ran the office, John maintained the records, and George managed the construction materials, but was not a member of EL&TCo. The fifth brother Charles, was very ill and died later in 1889 in Escondido.

Surveys began for the town and with two hills in the center of the development, the Escondido Hotel was constructed on the north hill. Having three stories, 100 rooms, and a view from the top of the hill, the hotel was designed to attract visitors to buy land. EL&TCo then kept a temporary sales office in the hotel.

From the hotel, downtown Escondido appeared to be a scat-

George V. Thomas

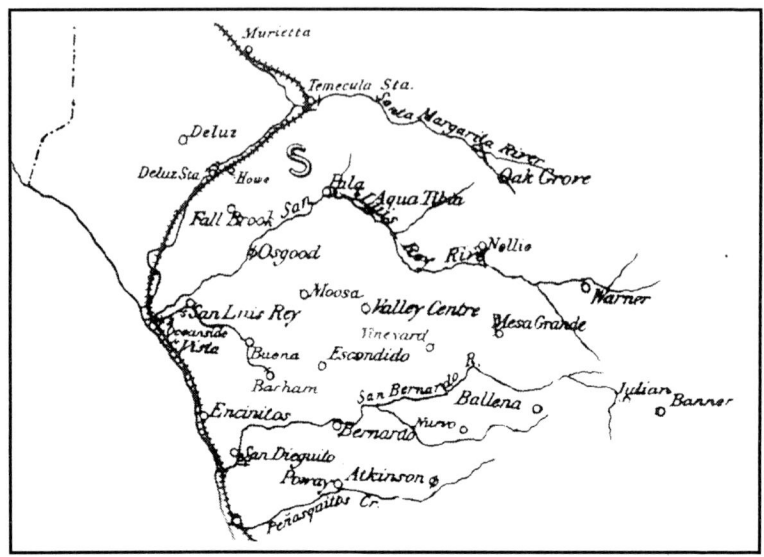

Map of Escondido prior to 1888.

tering of buildings with ranch lands in the distance. Roads criss-crossed the area, from point to point. Survey maps showed a town, but in reality few roads had been graded. The community was about to grow.

Activity ensued: wagons hauled in lumber, bricks were made by Chinese workers at the brickyard on west Grand Avenue, and the Escondido Post Office moved into town in a store on Grand Ave. The four Thomas brothers operated both sales offices, construction yards, and the hotel, and a model house was built. The Lime St. School was constructed and the bank was funded by two of the Thomas brothers and Jacob Gruendike. A newspaper started up: *The Escondido Times,* and to add to the well water, brick cisterns were lowered into the creek for a water supply.

The Escondido Land & Town Company had just erected a two-story building and opened a bank, but did not have the capital to proceed as planned. The company advertised nation wide for a buyer, and A. W. Wohlford, then living in the midwest, read the advertisement and was interested. He later came to Escondido,

This is the earliest known photograph of Escondido. Looking west down what would become Grand Ave. – 1886.

bought the building and the bank, and was prominent for many years in the financial development of the city.

Churches were offered free lots on which to build, and seven were constructed by 1900: Methodist Episcopal (1886), Baptist (1887), Southern Methodists (1887), Congregational (1888), Episcopal (1889), Roman Catholic (1893), and Christian (1900).

The University of Southern California had been founded by the Methodist Episcopal Church. In 1880, they began an expansion of branches in southern California, of which the Escondido branch was the fifth. These were feeder schools, to USC in Los Angeles, and referred to a colleges. They offered classes in a variety of subjects including languages: German, Latin, and Greek.

The Methodist Episcopal Church had brought the University of Southern California seminary to Escondido, and took good advantage of the land gift. Two blocks of 500 lots each, with alternating lots on either side of Grand Avenue, were given to USC. The lots were then sold to finance the school. Construction of the building began on the second hill, south of the hotel. The cost was $40,000, but the land they had been given was valued at $100,000.

EL&TCo then set up a sales office in San Diego and strung a 40 mile long telephone line from the office to the hotel. Opening day was set for March 29, 1886.

The first public excursion brought mostly speculators to Escondido, but upon returning to the San Diego office, they bought and sold land like they were trading stocks and bonds. The event was so successful that the first three day's receipts totaled a whopping $70,000. Still, families bought land too, and built homes.

The success of the operation prompted the

The Escondido USC Seminary College

Lime Street School and students – 1895.

California Southern Railroad to open a spur line at Steward Station in Leucadia, so wagons could bring people up to Escondido from there. The first event's revenues had been reserved however, to bring a railroad to the community, and that began the next year.

Having two members on the board of the San Diego Central Railroad allowed the company to acquire the charter, and the railroad to Escondido was started in March of 1887. EL&TCo then partnered with the San Marcos Land Company, who now owned the *Rancho Los Vallecitos de San Marcos,* and they co-funded the railroad line with $200,000. Many of the investors of EL&TCo were investors in the San Marcos Land Company. EL&TCo proposed a $50,000 bonus if the train arrived by the first of the year.

The San Diego Central's charter ran from San Diego to Oceanside however, it had been proposed to go up through the El Cajon Valley, to Poway, Bernardo, and Escondido. Tracks were laid to Escondido from the San Diego line, but up from Oceanside.

The bridge over the Escondido Creek had not been completed by December of that year. Wanting to win the $50,000 prize, the SDCR laid the tracks through the dry creek bed, to bring a train to Escondido on December 31st.

Plans for the first train excursion to Escondido went into effect. The Escondido Board of Trade was set up to foster new businesses and farms, and the Escondido train Depot was constructed. Everything was ready to receive new buyers.

Fifteen passenger cars, loaded with prospective citizens, arrived in February of 1888 — the peak of the California boom. Some 3,000 buyers attended the grand event. Free meals, musical bands, and a tent featuring displays of fruit were available. The event was such a great success, a second excursion train was planned for the Fourth of July, just five months away.

Grand Avenue was graded and a street car line set up, to reach from the train depot to the hotel. A farm was purchased and a show ranch was established by Richard Thomas. The ranch grew several different crops and had selections of grove trees planted. EL&TCo moved into the bank building and the San Marcos Land Co. moved in next door.

The street car ordered for the July 4th excursion train didn't arrive but, the 'Booster Train' came in on time. Wagons and buggies were used to bring the participants from the train depot to the hotel, and tours were planned to the Show Ranch. The Board of Trade had displays set up in a large tent and a 'Model House' had been constructed on Third Ave. Charles Thomas lived in this house until his death in 1889. A horse powered bus was set up, to bring people from the depot to the hotel each evening, in place of the street car.

The Booster Train was a success, and before the train went out, a sales office was operated from the back of the train. Town lots and ranch lands were sold in quantity and Escondido increased its population again, ten-fold from the previous decade.

The community had been laid out with the east-west roads as avenues, named for states of the US. A few avenues in the north end of town were named for presidents. The north-south roads were laid out as streets, named for the types of grove trees that were — or could be — grown in Escondido, along with flowering plants. These were alphabetized from east to west, from Ash to Upas. Upas is an unusual selection, being a south

The Barclay house was built in the late 1880s on the north side of 2nd Avenue, between Escondido Boulevard and Maple Street. It was a typical home of that period, having an outhouse, barns, vegetable garden and flowers.

American 'poison arrow' tree.

Although EL&TCo had purchased the entire 12,654 acres of the original *Rancho Rincón del Diablo,* the town was centered on 1,854 acres, surrounding the creek. Escondido was officially a town, but that was about to change.

Hauling grain in the late 1800s.

Escondido Stage – 1886

Decoration Day parade, on Grand Ave. – 1889.

Laying the cornerstone of the Bank of Escondido – 1886

EL&TCo tent, Graham & Steiners – 1888

Board of Trade display in the EL&TCo office – 1888

Thomas' Model House – 1889

The Methodist Episcopal, USC Seminary — 1880s

Grand Ave. looking east from Maple St. – 1889

Escondido – 1887

The Thomas Show Ranch

The George Thomas house on 5th Ave. at Kalmia St.

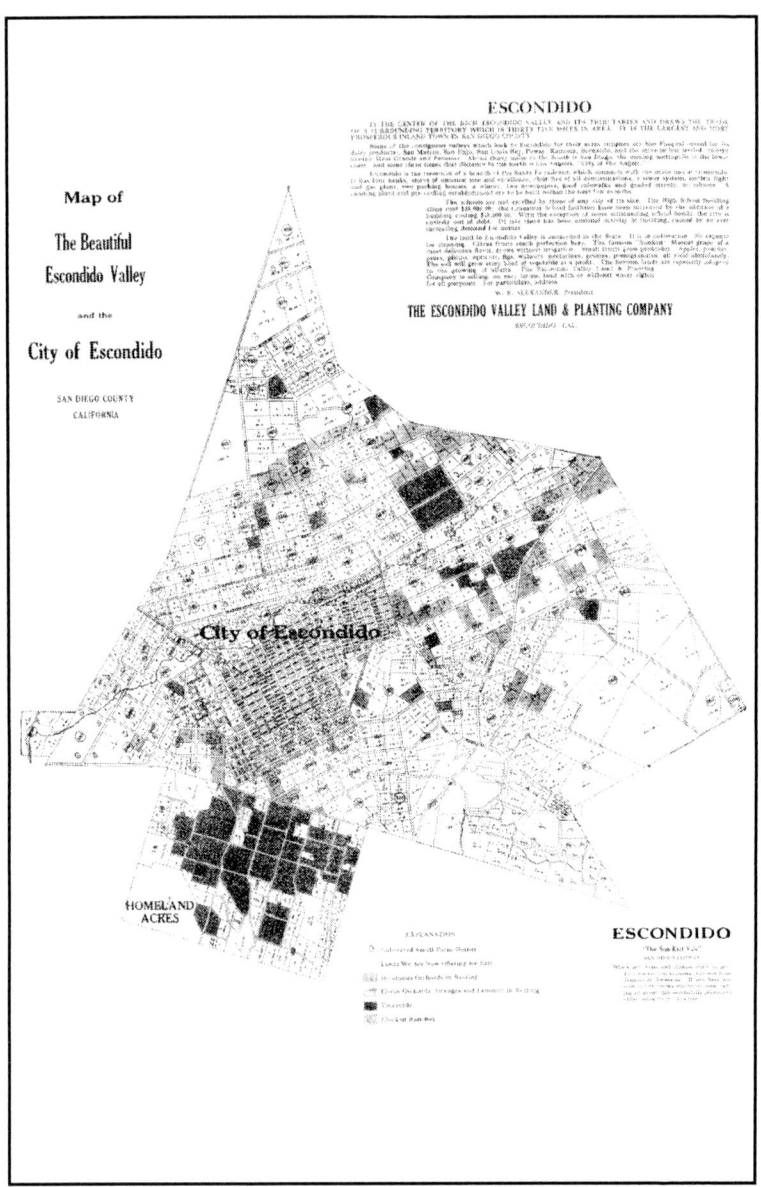

Map of Escondido

Chapter 4
THE CITY OF ESCONDIDO

"Escondido Muscat grapes test sweetest
in the State of California."
State Horticultural Report

Now having a bank, college, school, railroad, and a population of perhaps 500 souls, Escondido incorporated as a city on October 8, of 1888. Grand Avenue was the center of town, running between Ohio (now Valley Parkway) and Indiana (2nd Avenue.) People came by train, bringing all their belongings. Houses were built, and farms laid out: Escondido was growing.

The city was laid out with the outside boundaries of Grant (Mission) to Idaho (15th), and Ash (still Ash,) to Vine (still Vine.) Because of the two hills in town (the hotel and the college,) avenues east of the hills were numbered First Street through Eighth (now Pennsylvania through 6th.) Grand Avenue wound around the hotel going north, and Ivy Street became Curve Street around the college going east.

Southeast of the hotel and behind the college, avenues were numbered from First to Eighth. Chestnut Avenue was a diagonal from Minnesota southwest to Juniper Street, near Florida Avenue (13th.)

The alphabetical tree names for roads were used to encourage people to plant groves, and the U.S. State's names

Speer truck loading up at depot – 1900

Dixon Family – 1900

W.H. Baldridge house on 3rd Ave. – 1900

A. R. Moon Jewelry Store and Leo Escher Barber Shop on the 100 block of E. Grand Ave. – 1890

Bridge over Escondido Creek at Lime St. (Broadway) looking southeast – 1895

Mine Shaft #1, Cleveland Pacific Mine – 1896.

for roads were to inspire people to move here, so they could live on the street of their birthplace.

Escondido Creek ran north of Pennsylvania Avenue, and does today in a concrete culvert. It was the only water supply other than wells. Grapes were grown in abundance and Escondido became known for its produce throughout the state. Grapes were grown in Escondido since the 1860s, muscats since the 1880s. In the 1880s, these won state awards.

Escondido was the fourth city incorporated in what was San Diego county at the time; the county was reduced in size slightly in 1895, and in half during 1907. Oceanside was the third city in San Diego County, incorporating in 1888 as well. National City had done so the previous year and Coronado did so in 1890.

Grand Avenue was widened and boardwalks constructed, some 16 feet wide. Six coal-oil lamps lined Grand Avenue between Maple and Kalmia [a mountain laurel: *Kalmia Latifolia*.]

Oro Fino Mine – Hwy. 78 & Bear Valley – 1907

With Grand Avenue at 100 feet wide, and the street car never used, the tracks were pulled up.

The City Hall was constructed and a Court of the Township was founded, and an Escondido Board of Trustees was elected, with A. K. Cravath as the first president. A City Clerk, Treasurer and Marshal were also voted in; one of the Marshal's duties was to keep the six coal-oil lamps lit until midnight.

This was still the wild west — even to the visit of Wyatt Earp, who judged a horse race at the county fair the next year in Escondido. Also Sam Brannan, a millionaire — California's first, from San Francisco, died in Escondido unknown and broke. Others from the wild west came to town, and although the population boom was over, people continued to come to Escondido to live. Farmers, ranchers, and townspeople, arrived in Escondido by the carload, and built many homes still present in the historic district of town.

Judge Witherby's gold mine was still in operation — as were eighteen other claims. The Oro Fino mine and the Cleveland Pacific, each produced over $100,000 in gold — at $16 an ounce.

The national census in 1890, showed that there were 541 people in Escondido. A new school was started and the USC

View of Escondido from high school hill – 1905

Looking north from high school hill – 1900

Irrigating Boyle citrus grove – Oak Hill and Midway – 1900

*Hay baling east of the hotel (a rare view of the east side
of the hotel) – 1909*

Canal workers camp – 1894

Overlooking Escondido Dam and reservoir site – 1894

Seminary closed. The bond holder to the college, Henry Putnam, donated the building to the high school district, formed by a special vote. An agrarian newspaper began in town: *The Advocate.*

Agriculture was booming: 50,000 grove trees were planted, wheat for 1893 was up to 80,000 bushels and Escondido fruit won prizes at the Chicago Worlds Fair. Trains took out more than 180 carloads of produce and national markets began to open.

The year 1890 was a rainy year, well above average, and provided the community with surplus water. It was the last for over a decade and the years 1894, '96, '98, '99, and 1900 proved to be well below normal.

The drought condition caused the creation of the Escondido Irrigation District (EID) and $450,000 in water bonds was proposed for dam construction. A vast lake was to be created up in Bear Valley — aptly named for the grizzly bears once seen in the vicinity. (The last grizzly bear in California was killed in 1921.)

The plan was to bring water from the San Luis Rey river up north, to the dam site in Bear Valley, creating a large reservoir. Lake Escondido would then, through a gravity fed system, bring

Midday rest at upper camp – 1894

The Blacksmith Shop at Hell Hole camp – 1894

The Finishers – 1894

Work on the canal – 1894

water to the townsite and the water system there at Park Hill. Water from the river however, belonged to the Native Americans.

The bonds were approved and were quickly sold, and the EID began dam construction in 1894. The city's water system was purchased, and crews were hired. The dam was built by man and mule.

A redwood frame was constructed to hold the rock fill, and at completion, the dam was 76 feet high. To feed the reservoir, a 15 mile long canal had to be constructed, north to the river. Eight work camps were built, including the dam site where 75 men were housed. The main camp was called Hell Hole, and it held the blacksmith's shop and lumber fabrication mill, used to support the other camps.

As the dam was started, the canal was begun as well. Built in stages, different crews followed each other, from each of the eight camps: doing blasting, roughing, finishing, trestle construction, and flume millwork.

The project took just under a year to complete. On July 5th in 1895, water flowed for the first time, from Lake Escondido.

The city of Escondido finally had its own irrigation system. The EID had done its job, at the cost of $350,000.

The water however, came from the San Luis Rey river. This was on reservation land and was never legally obtained. The Native Americans had been deprived of a badly needed resource and did not receive reparation until a century later. It was the Luíseño Indians who spent the better part of the last half of the 20th century fighting for their cause.

Even with a national recession, the banks in Escondido did not close. Overdue mortgages however, caused landowners to give up their

Escondido Land & Town Company office – 1887

First Public Library built 1895 on Grand Ave. & Valley St. – 1910

property and new homes were not built in town for five years.

The Chamber of Commerce was started, with the name change from the Board of Trade, and they moved over to Grand Ave. One of the Thomas Brothers gave up the hotel to the manager, and moved to Los Angeles, and another sold the Show Ranch.

Of significant note, the Escondido Library opened down the hill from the High School, on Grand, just east

Mina Ward, first Librarian – 1895

of Ivy, with Mina Ward as the first Librarian. Over 300 books were donated — some of which were considered objectionable.

It took five years for the reservoir to fill up, and during that

The flume – 1894

time, animals tunneled into the dirt canals, flumes began leaking, and ditches required concrete linings. Operational costs increased and little more than half of the water from the San Luis Rey river ever reached the reservoir.

By 1900 however, Escondido had 755 people. There was still no electricity, nor gas to the homes, but eighteen telephones had been installed. One improvement was that the six coal-oil streetlights on Grand Avenue were changed over to gaslights — relieving the marshal of one responsibility.

The reservoir at Lake Escondido overflowed, and water was plentiful. Payments on the water bonds however, came due, and many farmers felt they would lose their lands and so wouldn't pay their water taxes. Others simply couldn't pay, or gave up their land and left town. EL&TCo stopped paying on the taxes on lands they still owned, and one year, only $435 was collected in water tax.

The interest owed on the bonds mushroomed to $137,000, and $530,000 in total was due. With people selling out and moving away — even two of the Thomas Brothers, Escondido was a solemn place in which to live.

The Escondido Irrigation District then struck a deal with

Escondido Reservoir and dam – 1910

Grand Ave. looking west – 1890

the bonds holder: the bonds would be relinquished if the EID could pay 43¢ on the dollar. This left $228,585 due. The EID levied an assessment on all real property in the district. The assessment was paid by each landowner as a contribution on a purely voluntary basis. The bondholders foreclosed on all the property within the old rancho boundary: 12,654 acres. Then an auction was held and the water district bought back the land with the funds contributed by the landowners.

The Escondido Mutual Water Company (EMCW) was then formed to replace the EID. Those owners who had made contributions were given their land back. Those who had not, had their land turned over to the EMWC.

The landowners received one share of stock in the new company for every dollar they had contributed. And those shares entitled them to water rights. The water bonds were paid off on October 31, 1904 and a celebration was due for Escondido.

Grand Ave looking east from Maple – 1905

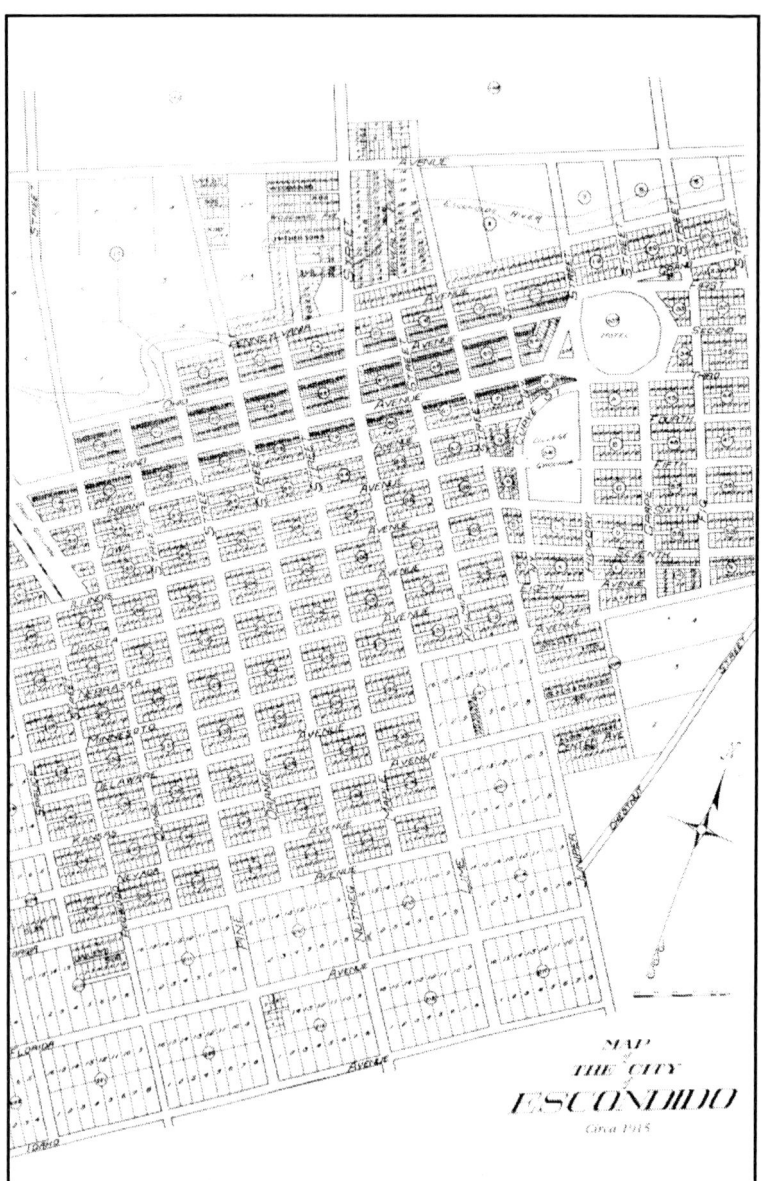

Map of Escondido in 1915, showing the original street names

Chapter 5
THE TURN OF A NEW CENTURY

"Cheers rent the air; men tossed their hats and
hurrahed; women waved their handkerchiefs. It
was a cheering, shouting throng that yelled
itself hoarse with wild enthusiasm."
The Los Angeles Times – Sept. 9, 1905

While the turn of the new century actually happened a few years before, the turn for Escondido occurred on the 9th of September in 1905. This was designated *'Bond Burning Day.'* The water bonds had been paid off the previous October, however, an event was needed to celebrate the financial freedom of the farming community. California's Admissions Day was selected as the day of celebration.

This was to be a big event as it was a great accomplishment for the citizens of Escondido to pay off $228,000 in water bonds, especially just after a national recession. Once the day was selected, plans for the celebration were under way for months. This was to be both a celebration for the people of Escondido, and a trade event for farmers to show off their produce to the visiting public.

Promotion for the festivities was throughout southern California, and another excursion train from San Diego was scheduled. The Chamber of Commerce took full advantage of the opportunity and organized displays of produce. Booths were setup, the Woman's Relief Corps and several of the church groups organized food displays.

The train came in at 9:00 am bringing people to Escondido to help celebrate the event. Horse and buggys went to the train station, just to meet the visiting guests. The Escondido Coronet band started to play, along with the San Diego City Guard band, and they marched up Grand Avenue from the station.

Grape Day arriving at the Depot – 1908

The street itself was decked out in red, white, and blue bunting, with a banner stretched across the street proclaiming: FREEDOM. Visitors and citizens alike, marched in the self-made parade, where wagons and people went side-by-side up Grand. The main gathering was in front of the Lime Street School, at 2:30 in the afternoon. Music was plentiful, with a speech by Judge J. N. Turrentine.

At 4:15, the bonds hanging from a wire basket, were lit. As the paper bonds went up in smoke, cheers, hats, and handkerchiefs went up into the air. The blazing basket was raised above the heads of the spectators.

A sudden mishap occurred when the rope holding the burning bonds caught fire: the entire basket fell to the ground.

Freedom parade to the water bond burning – 1905

Everyone scattered and a few men surrounded the flaming documents, holding hands in a circle to protect women and children. They did not however, try to stop the fire. They wanted

Bond burning celebration at the Lime Street School – 1905

to ensure the entire basket of bonds burned entirely into: 'The ashes of prosperity.'

Escondido was free — free of the financial weight of the water bonds, which was expressed on that banner over Grand Avenue, and throughout the city: Freedom. Water however, was still plentiful in Escondido. With the reservoir full and the canal operating, the town and the farming community could proceed to grow. Water that was the source of their new-found prosperity, and the foundation of the agriculture in grains, citrus, and most importantly, grapes.

Fishing off Bear Valley Dam (aka Lake Wohlford)

Escondido was growing and the little hamlet of 1888 was now almost 18 years old with a population of over 1,000 souls. Steiner and Company operated the general store, Stevenson Brothers were clothiers and also sold groceries, dry goods, and hardware; The Bank of Escondido which had been bought out by A. W. Wohlford more than a decade earlier, was still the largest brick building on Grand Avenue.

Escondido reservoir and dam

Still, much of Escondido was rural. Being an agrarian community, farms covered most of the city, from hills to hills. The original grant boundary had taken advantage of the flat lands: most of the land inside the city was level ground. The

Four wagons leaving town, in front of the Bank of Escondido.

hills were reserved for groves of fruit bearing trees — citrus fruit which would one day be one of the best selling crops.

Over the years, grains gave way to citrus. Higher value and ease of cultivation, brought many citrus types and labels. Packing houses evolved and trainloads of oranges, lemons, and other tree bearing fruit, were shipped out regularly. Grapes however, had been in the valley since the 1860 and were still the reputation of Escondido.

Inside a citrus packing house

Grape cultivation increased. Every year, the people of Escondido continued to celebrate Admission Day and the burning of the bonds. In 1908, the chairman of the board of trustees (now mayor,) proposed to change 'Bond Burning Day' to 'Grape Day,' in celebration of Escondido's bountiful grape harvest. A Grape Day committee was formed, and an event logo designed; September 9th of 1908 was officially proclaimed Grape Day.

Excursion trains were well known in Escondido, dating from 1888. This time was no different. The train pulled in in the morning and 1,100 people came to tour the farms and see the parade.

Grand Avenue was decked out in banners and booths, each showing off the successes of the city. A hot air balloon offered rides, and grapes were given away by the car load. Grape Day was official, and would continue throughout the years.

The years 1909 and 1910, were much the same: the train arrived and essentially a farmers market was put on display. Grapes on ice, were available at the Pioneer Meat Market on West Grand Avenue. After

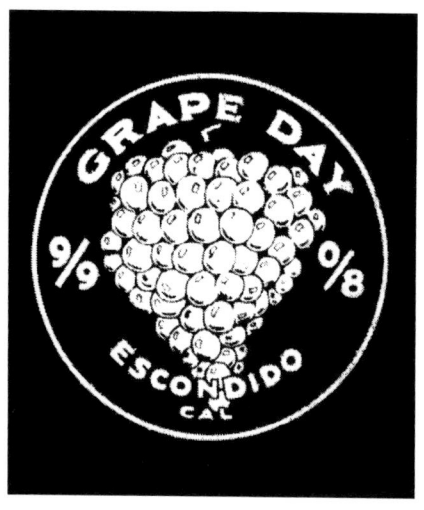

Logo for Grape Day – 1908.

Grape Day Committee in front of the crowd – 1908

Pioneer Meat Market decorated for Christmas – 1900

1907, the market had its own steam driven ice maker.

In 1911 however, the celebration moved to a new location, the site of the former Lime Street School. The school had been deemed unsafe, so the school board had it torn down in 1909, and a new school built on Fifth Avenue in 1910. This left open land for a park which was used for the annual festival.

Parades continued to be held, and the next year proved to be even a bigger success. A Grape Day Queen was chosen in 1913, and she road on her parade 'float,' through town — an automobile decked out in flowers. With each succeeding year, other events were added: stunt flying, motorcycle races, and baseball games. Grapes were given away to the tune of 20,000 pounds.

The Lime Street School had started in 1886, yet for the children too far out of town, Oak Glen and Rincon (formerly Hiddendale up in Reidy Canyon,) held class up to fifth grade. Oak Glen burned in 1904. All students then went to Escondido High School. Grades six through twelve were housed in the big

1st Grape Day Queen, Margaret Juny – 1913

Grape wagon advertising FREE GRAPES

Rincon Elementary School – 1906

brick former college building, up on the hill. Many walked to school, some rode a horse, a few rode in a buggy. A few went barefoot.

Taking a donkey to school.

Grades 6-12 at Escondido High School – 1906

Orange Glen School – 8th Grade Graduation – 1942

Male students hand dug the Escondido High School swimming pool – 1912

Horse and mule were the mode of transportation of the day, from buggys and trims, to carriages and wagons — everything moved by four-legged animal. With the railroad in town since 1888, Speer's Truck and Transport hauled everything from dry goods and machinery, to personal items.

The year 1906 brought 93 automobiles to Escondido. On the trail of an endurance run from Los Angeles to San Diego, Escondido was one of the stops.

In 1909, a Rally for Roads bond was promoted throughout San Diego county. One million dollars was being asked to provide road improvements, county wide. Escondido citizens knew the importance of accessibility for the automobile, and joined in.

Speer Transfer Co. wagon – 300 block of east Grand Ave – c. 1910

A road race through town was held in 1913 from San Diego to Los Angeles, with a $100 prize. A Fiat won, with a local Escondido Ford coming in sixth place. The purpose was promotional — to get people to buy cars.

Buy cars they did, merchants in town, farmers in the field, just about everyone was buying a car. As cars became popular in town, gasoline to operate them was initially scarce. Private gas tanks of up to 500 gallons could be found at homes and

Rally for Roads – 1909

businesses, (sometimes buried in the lawn,) even smaller portable tanks were used in town.

For the farming community, things were booming. Water was plentiful, crops were increasing, and everything shipped out by train. There were many citrus packing houses as citrus was now king, and in season, the railroad left every day.

Although much still moved by horse and wagon, it was well

Escondido Garage – 206 W. Grand Ave. – 1914

Three Escondido businesses with a portable gas pump beside the curb – c. 1915

evident that the automobile was taking over. The livery stable was now also the local garage, and passenger stages were now cars. Auto garages were auto dealers as well.

Loveless Orange Packing House – 2nd Ave. & Spruce St.– 1915

Escondido Depot – Grand Ave. & Spruce St. – 1910

As early as 1912, the City of San Diego had considered hiring Charles M. Hatfield, commonly known as the *Rainmaker,* due to county wide drought conditions. Hatfield had seen success in Los Angeles and in the great valley of California, in providing rain for drought burdened farmers. In late 1915, Hatfield was ready to provide rain.

By the second week of January, 1916, it was raining, by the

New Palace Livery & Garage – 2nd Ave. & Kalmia St. – c. 1912

15th it was a downpour. Nearly 20 inches fell on Escondido alone, and by the end of the month, water was pouring over the Bear Valley dam. Buildings collapsed, railroads torn up, and homes were inundated.

Flood damage west of Grape Day Park – 1916

Railroad tracks damaged by flood, south of Washington Ave. – 1916

A damaged house on the 100 block of West Valley – 1916

Nearly every bridge in San Diego county was washed out, including the Bernardo bridge. The following year the Bernardo dam was started, which would eventually flood the town of Bernardo with Lake Hodges. A few years later, the Bernardo bridge was rebuilt.

Lake Hodges Bridge, (Bernardo Bridge) looking south – c. 1919

World War I was on the horizon and when the United States entered the war in 1917, the Bear Valley dam was sabotaged. Previously, the water level at the reservoir had been elevated with redwood planking at the spillway. Dynamite blew away the planks and water streamed out of the dam. After that, a 24 hour guard was installed, with fencing and lights.

Calvary units of the US Army, were stationed at Kearny Mesa in south county. Military exercises, brought troops through the streets of Escondido. Citizens bought Liberty Bonds to support the war effort, and people were asked to collect peach pits, walnut shells, and bones to be burned and used as charcoal filters for gas masks. All of the bones in Dead Horse Canyon were taken during the war effort.

Armistice Day brought cheers to the streets of Escondido, with a parade as a giant American flag was carried down Grand Avenue. Speeches were given in Grape Day Park, and the school bell rang most of the night.

Bear Valley Lake was renamed Lake Wohlford in 1924 when Alvin W. Wohlford died. He had been a great contributor to both Escondido and the water system for many years.

WWI horse artillery from Camp Kearny on Grand Ave. NE of Broadway – 1918

Felicita

The story of Felicita was originally told in Elizabeth Judson Roberts' book *Indian Stories of the South West*, published in 1917. Felicita lived in San Pasqual valley.

As a young girl, she was baptized by the Padres from San Diego, and given the name Felicita. During the Mexican-American war, the Mexican army came to her village, frightening the Native Americans away. Led by General Andres Pico, brother of Governor Pio Pico, the army camped in their village, using their huts for shelter and their food for sustanance.

Afraid by the actions of the Mexicans, the villagers were cautious in returning to their homes. After some time, the American army came, and battled with the Mexicans. The American's, led by General Steven Kearny, were held in position overnight. Acording to Felicita, her father Pontho, led two of the Americans to San Diego to gather reinforcements. Pontho was the leader of their tribe.

Felicita told that during the battle, an American soldier was wounded by a lone Mexican, and left to die. She came to the man and using his cap, brought water for him and dressed his wound with leaves — in the Native American way. She then got help from her family, who told the other Americans of the wounded soldier. They in turn, came and brought him back to safety.

Sometime later having healed somewhat, the soldier returned to her village, speaking with her for some time. Eventually he left, leaving Felicita with a broken heart over her soldier that she had saved.

Local optometrist Benjamin Sherman, wrote the Felicita Pageant in 1927, which ran for five years. Stopped by the depression, the play has been revived several times since. During the early days of the play's run, a park was developed for the presentation. Felicita Park, located south of the town center, is more than 50 acres in size and offers other recreational activities.

The Felicita Pageant – 1927-1931

WWI Victory Parade on Grand Ave. – 1918

The local economy was based upon the export of agriculture and much of that was still grapes. Prohibition went into effect after the war, lasting almost 14 years from the start of 1920 to the end of 1933. Many of the vineyards and wineries changed over to citrus

Eureka Ranch – Valley Blvd. & Washington Ave. – 1913

Packing house crew of the Escondido Fruit Growers Association – Valley & Quince Ave. – 1910

and started groves in avocados.

Yet, illegal distillation plants were found in the area. Bootlegger's shipped out barrels of alcohol, and Federal agents caught many of them. During this time, the original Escondido Hotel was torn down, but the Charlotta Hotel on Upas Street, and the Logan Hotel in town, provided overnight comfort. The high school (College building,) was also taken down after it had been destroyed by fire. The new high school was built just south of the old one, still up on the hill.

Even with Prohibition in force, life was good in Escondido. More businesses came to town, an apartment house was con-

Confiscated still

Hotel Charlotta – 1930

Escondido High School construction – 4th Ave. & Hickory St. – 1927

★ The Turn of a New Century ★

Trenton Apartment, Escondido's first apartment building – 200 E. 2nd Ave. – c. 1915

Escondido Steam Laundry crew – 126 W. Grand Ave. – c. 1929

Busy Bee Cash Grocery – 200 block N. Broadway – c. 1928

structed, and the local Escondido Baseball team was doing well.

The original signal light at the intersection of Grand and Lime (Broadway today,) was replace by a 100-foot tall flagpole — right in the middle of the intersection. This was on Flag day, June 14, 1927; the police department was responsible for raising

Escondido Baseball Team – 1925

Finney Field #1, first baseball field with lights – Woodward & Escondido

and lowering the flag each day.

The long standing Board of Trustees was replaced by a City Council in 1928 with the chairman of the board becoming the mayor. The Marshall became the chief of police and the fire bell at the fire station was replaced with a new siren.

The center of Grand Ave. at Broadway, with light pole – c. 1920 and with flagpole in 1927.

Escondido was becoming a modern city, and it had gas and electricity to most homes and businesses. The Escondido Utilities Company generated electricity locally.

The Fifth Avenue school continued to be the grade school, central to the community, and a newly commissioned, gas powered school bus brought the children each day. Children still however, came dressed as they were — town kids dressed up,

Volunteer Firemen & truck – Grape Day Park – 1926

Escondido Utilities Co. – 3rd Ave. & Spruce St. – 1911

Interior of Escondido Utilities Co. – 1911

farm kids in overalls — many still barefoot.

While the Great Depression caused many to lose their jobs, farmers persevered to produce their citrus crops, and the packing houses stayed open. Grape Day, still an annual event, continued

5th Avenue School – 100 block of 5th Ave.

7th & 8th Grade class at 5th Avenue School – 1927

Students from 5th Avenue School in costume – 1928

Elementary class at 5th Avenue School – 1924

Escondido grammar school bus outside 5th Ave. School – c. 1922

to support the farmers. The celebration showed off their produce, and gave the citizens a feeling of prosperity.

Trucks of course had replaced wagons by this time, and cars were used instead of horse and buggy; but only if gasoline was

Interior of Escondido Lemon Assoc. packing house – 220 N. Tulip St. – 1936

Escondido Lemon Assoc. packing house – 220 N. Tulip St. – c. 1930

Escondido Orange Assoc. & ice house – 1155 W. Mission Ave. – c. 1950

Escondido Line Crew (SDG&E) – 3rd Ave. & Spruce St. – c. 1930

available. Gas stations had started to show up, first within the car dealerships, then later as independent businesses. Yet, supply was a problem because of the economy.

The cost of everyday items made it difficult for many people to just get by. Although the prices of the day seem low by today's standards, some things were just too expensive to purchase.

Grape Day continued on through the depression. During the early 1930s, a miniature golf course was set up in Grape

Stafford Chevrolet Co. – 208 N. Broadway Ave – 1933

Luke's Golden State Service Station – 649 N. Broadway Ave. – 1930

Day Park. Citrus displays were always included in the Grape Day celebration and avocados were introduced. Of course grapes were always on display and available in great quantities, to give away.

Inside of Jenness Groceries – 1935

Miniature golf course set up for Grape Day – 1930

Grape Day grape display – 1930

In 1910, a new Carnegie Library was constructed at 3rd Ave. and Kalmia St., replacing the original library on Grand Avenue.

The Carnegie foundation provided a library grant of $7,500, and the city was required to fund 10% of the grant each year, toward library operations.

Although the United States had been in preparation for WWII, the attack on Pearl Harbor in December of 1941, followed with the U.S. declaration of war on Japan and then Germany.

Men were recruited by the thousands; in total, 16 million men served throughout the war. Servicemen traveled mostly by trains and those leaving Escondido were no different. The first

Carnegie Library – 3rd. Ave.. & Kalmia St. – 1938

Grand Ave. looking west from Escondido Hotel – 1910

military unit stationed in Escondido were bivouacked in Grape Day Park.

Engel Field airport, was constructed north of Washington during the war, (operating up until 1954.) Because of the damage to the dam at Lake Wohlford, during WWI, a round-the-clock guard was installed.

Rationing started, using coupons and tokens — gasoline: 1942, sugar: 1942, coffee: 1943, meat: 1943, butter and cheese: 1943; and shoes — 3 pair a year. The city's main celebration, Grape Day occurred in 1940 and 1941, but was suspended for the duration of the war in 1942.

The end of WWII, brought the service men back, nation wide,

Engel Air Field – 1947

some 400,000 did not return. This brought prosperity to the community, new houses, new jobs, and new businesses — many based upon the automobile.

Grape Day continued, in 1947. Better crops with bigger yields were shown off at the farmer's market displays at Grape Day.

WWII troop train – Grand Ave. & Spruce St.

WWII guard at Lake Hodges Dam – 1942

WWII mess line in Grape Day Park – 1942

WWII Navy Mother's Hostess House – 1944

Grape Day Queen and court on parade float – 1941

The parade continued on Grand Avenue, with the Queen holding court on a float, and the crowds returned to Grape Day Park.

Mighetto Winery float in the Grape Day Parade – 1940

Luke's Golden State Service, Grape Day Float – 1947

Grape Day crowds in the park – 1947

Two remarkable events occurred during 1949: it snowed in Escondido during January, and Highway 395, *a freeway,* came through town in May of that year.

Grape Day Parade, Escondido High School Band – N. Broadway – 1947

Grape Day Parade Queen Float – 1949

★ The Turn of a New Century ★

The year of 1950, brought a close to the now famous Grape Day celebrations. The shift away from agriculture as an industry, and the building of homes on farm lands, helped to cause the demise of the 40+ year tradition. A brief revival of the event occurred during the 1970s, but it was not until 1996, that Grape Day finally permanently returned to Escondido.

Snow on citrus groves – 1949

New Highway 395 – looking south just before Grand Ave. – 1949

Appreciate Escondido's heritage and the Grape Day celebration, by taking the walking tour in downtown Escondido. This tour revisits many of the original historic buildings from the original town center, which then leads to the Escondido History Center in Grape Day Park.

Nelson's Market – N. Broadway & Washington

Chamber of Commerce – 499 S. Escondido Blvd. – 1951

Car Hop – 314 E. Grand Ave – 1945

Escondido Tractor Co. – 200 W. Grand Ave. – 1947

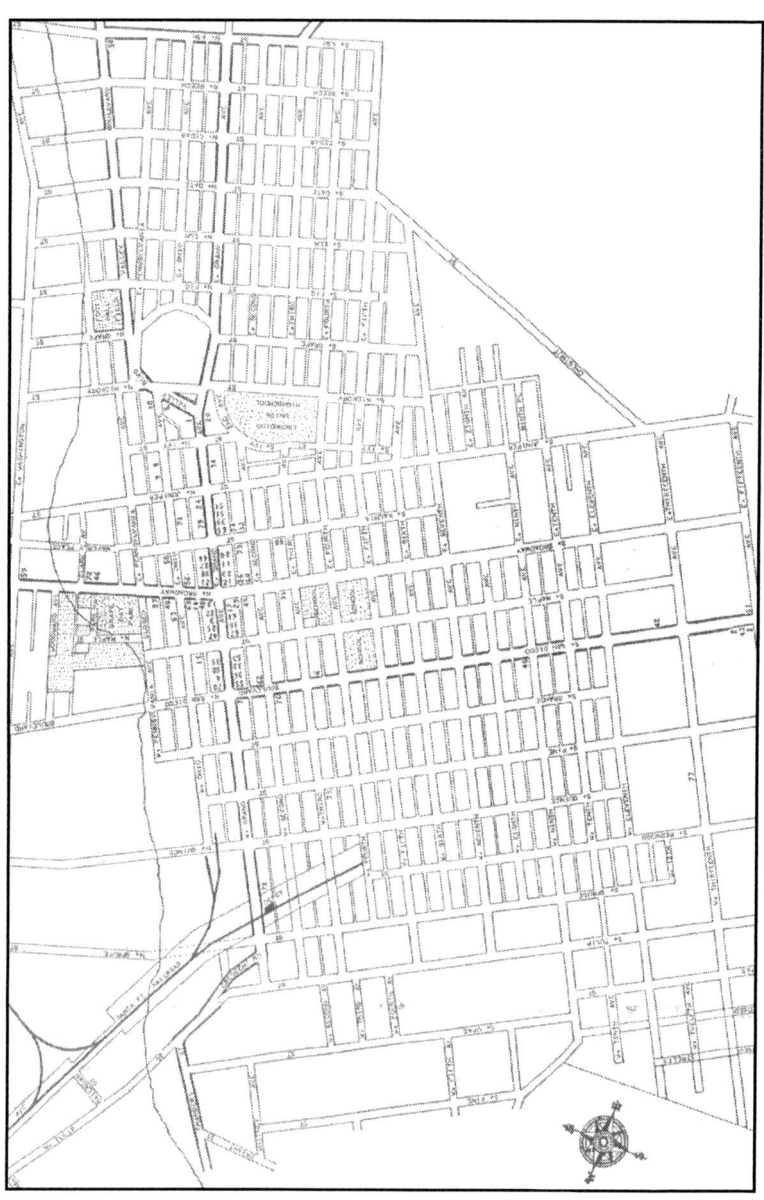

This map from 1938 shows the new street names – changed in 1930.

Chapter 6
ESCONDIDO HERITAGE &
THE GRAPE DAY CELEBRATION

Escondido Heritage Walking Tour
Grape Day Celebration
The Escondido History Center

Explore Escondido on a walking tour of historic downtown. Start at the corner of Grand Avenue and Broadway. This is the heart of downtown, where all street names change from East to West, and North to South.

It should also be acknowledged that Escondido was the center for the surrounding communities of North San Diego County. For instance, students attended Escondido High School not only from Escondido, but also Valley Center, San Marcos, Rancho Bernardo and Poway. Therefore, downtown Escondido served not only its own residents, but was also an economic center for the surrounding area.

Escondido High School at 4th Ave. and Hickory St. – c. 1945

Imagine the corner of Grand Ave. and Broadway Street decades ago. On the northwest corner is 102 W. Grand Avenue. Built in 1886, it is Grand Avenue's oldest existing structure. Originally The Bank of Escondido it was designed by San Diego architects Comstock & Trotsche in the Italianate style. Constructed of bricks made locally at a brickyard further east on Grand Avenue (with Chinese laborers), the building also housed the office of the Escondido Land & Town Company. A year after it was constructed the building was expanded

Bank of Escondido – NW corner of Grand at Broadway

on the east side. The first board sidewalks in the city were installed in front of the Bank of Escondido. The building sported a dome and cupola and several second-story bay windows, but has been remodeled several times over the decades.

Bank of Escondido on the right - looking west from the high school hill

Across the street on the southwest corner was Graham and Steiner's large two-story brick store. Graham & Steiner's was the first store in Escondido. Their brick store replaced their earlier wooden building that had been farther down block. Eagle Hall, which was used for dances and meetings, took up the entire 2nd floor, but was removed in 1960. A number of other Grand Avenue buildings were also taken down to one story over the years, mostly due to liability concerns due to their unreinforced brick construction.

Graham & Steiner's first store, 100 block west of Grand Ave. – 1894

Across Broadway on the southeast corner is a remodeled 1905 bank building. It had many name changes before it became the Bank of America. The door originally was on the corner of the building facing the intersection, as did the Bank of Escondido diagonally across the street. Dr. Buell had his dentist office on the second floor for many years.

First National Bank on SE corner of Grand at Broadway

Ting's Pharmacy was located on the northeast corner. It was a popular gathering place from 1928 to 1968.

Looking east on Grand Ave. & Broadway – Ting's Pharmacy was on the NE corner

A large flagpole graced the center of the road 1927 to 1944. The 90' tall flagpole was erected by the Consuelo Lodge of Masons as a gift to the city. The 90' tall pole had a concrete base smack dab in the middle of the street.

Flagpole at Grand Ave. & Broadway

This picture shows the base of the flagpole in the middle of the intersection.

The base was encased in a cement cone to protect it from vehicles. The city maintained the pole and the Escondido Police Department was in charge of raising and lowering the flag each day. It was taken down in 1944 due to its deteriorating condition and increased traffic, which made it a hazard.

Palm trees were planted to guide visitors from the Santa Fe Depot to downtown. They marched down Grand Avenue as far as Maple. In 2002 the city of Escondido replaced the original Washingtonian palms that had been planted in the 1914 (some say 1908) by the Floral Society, due to age and disease.

Grand Ave. looking west

This tour, for the most part, stays on Grand Ave.
Go west, on the south side of the street.

145 W. Grand Ave. — This was the site, on the second floor, of Escondido's first hospital.

The father and son physician team, the doctors Larzalere performed minor surgery here, using the even northern light. There was no elevator so patients presumably had to be able to walk up the stairs prior to surgery. The facade was covered with aluminum siding for many years, which has since been removed.

Look across the street and notice the dentil moldings that top many buildings on the street, in several slightly different styles. 126, 130 and 132 West Grand were built in the 1920s. The commercial style buildings feature stepped-back brick cornice and transoms (high windows) above the metal awnings. Most of the transoms on the street are now covered, but they were used to bring daylight deep into the buildings.

The Humpty Dumpty Market at 101 W. Grand Ave. – c. 1932

155 W. Grand Ave. — Built in the J. C. Penney corporate style, it housed the popular store until a large mall was built in 1986. The building then sat vacant for 17 years until being renovated and opening as a museum.

Cross to the north side of the street and go east.

100 block of W. Grand, including the first J.C. Penney Store

120 W. Grand Ave. — This was the location of the Logan Hotel, built in 1912. It provided rooms for business travelers upstairs and shop space at street level.

The commercial vernacular style was completely remodeled in the 1980s.

Miller's Cafe crew with Logan Hotel in the background – c. 1929

114 W. Grand Ave. — The Escondido Times occupied 114 W. Grand from 1886 until it merged with The Advocate in 1909. The Times was a weekly newspaper that trumpeted the merits of the region to lure more settlers. Its purpose was more to develop the area, than to serve it directly.

In the 1960s this was the location of Hoffmann's Pharmacy, which had an old fashioned soda fountain.

106-110 W. Grand Ave. — Built in 1887 in the Queen Anne style, to harmonize with the neighboring bank building on the corner. At times it and the bank have looked like one building, and at other times one or the other has been remodeled so they looked like two very distinct buildings. Note the entry tiles, tin ceiling, and original Escondido brick interior wall. Pioneer leaders met and governed the fledging city in a 2nd floor room until 1893.

The corner bank building was constructed in 1886 and expanded the following year along Grand Ave.

Cross Broadway

116 E. Grand Ave. — This is the location of the Princess Theatre. Built in 1914 with a sloped floor and a projection loft, it was Escondido's first real movie house. It became a billiard hall in the 1920s after the Kinema Theatre opened down the street at 207 E. Grand Ave.

The Kinema Theater – 200 block E Grand – c. 1930

122 E. - This was built in 1909 and operated as The Commercial Hotel. The lobby and dining room were in the first floor east bay and upstairs housed traveling salesmen. Cassous' Pioneer Meat Market occupied the west front part of the building.

Pioneer Meat Market with iced grapes for Grape Day – 1909

130 E. Grand Ave. — Alonzo Moon built this building around 1890 for his watch repair and jewelry store. Moon was also the city's official weather ob-server from 1894 to 1935. He used a rain gauge and thermom-eter put in the yard of his shop by the United States Weather Bureau to meticulously record Escondido's tem-perature and rain-fall. When the build-ing was remodeled in the 1950s it lost its original Victorian detailing.

Alonzo Moon's Jewelry Store – 1890

132-36-38 E. Grand Ave. — This was the site of Leo Escher's Barber Shop. Escher arrived in the 1880s and was Escondido's first real barber and also served as drum major for the community's band.

140-142 E. Grand Ave. — A hardware store operated here for over 70 years. After opening in 1897 it had several different names until around 1922 when Arthur Churchill bought

Leo Escher's Barber Shop – c. 1890

into the existing partnership of Andrew Robertson and Mathew

Interior of the Escondido Hardware Store – 100 block E. Grand – c. 1910

Cassou. When Robertson died Churchill became manager and the final name was established: Churchill & Cassou's Hardware Store. It closed in 1968.

146-158 E. Grand Ave. — Now divided into several stores, this was built circa 1890 for the Stevenson Bros. general merchandise store, which also sold groceries. The Escondido brick building had a second floor with fraternal meeting rooms. The entire 2nd floor was later removed, and eventually the stairway entrance (to the left of 146) was disguised to look like a clock. The original brick, which has been sandblasted, is exposed on the exterior wall facing Kalmia.

Stevenson Bros. wagon – c. 1895

Cross Kalmia

200 E. Grand Ave. — Built circa 1940, this was an Art Deco style gas station. The original streamlined facade is intact.

218 E. Grand Ave. — The Arcade building was built in 1946. The design was a new concept when it was designed here. It has a Moderne pent roof and metal signage. After the building was constructed the Elks met on the 2nd floor. The hardwood floors in the assembly room were designed for dancing.

224 E. Grand Ave. — Originally built in two sections with an open lot between the two, this was the location of Oscar Hall's garage and Ford dealership. Beginning in 1941 it was the site of the Homer Heller Ford agency and service center. When Highway 395 opened in 1949 Heller Ford moved to the corner of Grand at 395, which later became Centre City Parkway.

Homer Heller Ford Agency 224 E. Grand Ave. – c. 1948

240-252 E. Grand Ave. — The Patio Shops, built around an open arcade, opened in 1946. The design is similar to the Arcade Building down the street, but is not under one roof.

262 E. Grand Ave. — Safeway built this in 1936. The building was a grocery store for most of its life.

Shelby's Food Market, occupied the site until 1972. It is designed in the Streamlined Moderne style with fluted pilasters and a decorative cornice and transoms.

Safeway Store – during the Grape Day Parade 1940

Shelby's Grocery – at the corner of Grand Ave. and Kalmia

Cross Juniper

326 E. Grand Ave. — This is an Art Deco gem. Built in 1938 it has the original metal casement windows, a pent roof over the door, fluted columns and incised reveals that accent the horizontal elements of the design.

Cross to the south side of the street between Hickory and Ivy.

A row of 5 iron rings are embedded along the curb. They were used to tie up horses. Horse rings remain in several places in the city, but this location has the largest number all together.

Cross Ivy and go east on the south side of the street.

333 E. Grand Ave. — This was an A&P store that later became the landmark Big E market. It was built in 1949. The soaring pylon that displayed the logo, and the liberal use of glass brick were contemporary features.

317 E. Grand Ave. — The black tiles of vitreous glass and cantilevered upper-story showcase are the special features of this 1948 building. It was built as a furniture store.

309 E. Grand Ave. — C.A. Balch, who specialized in theaters, designed the Ritz Theatre. It was built in 1937 in the Zigzag Moderne style; it has very sculptural shapes and angled metal accents. The movie theatre opened with "Broadway Melody of 1938." Originally a mural was above the marquee. The building was later gutted by fire.

301 E. Grand Ave. — This companion building to the theatre began in 1937 as the Grand Market. This intersection has had a grocery store on 3 of the 4 corners at one time or another. The Grand Market, however, was the first market in Escondido with grocery carts.

Look south from the corner of Grand and Juniper to Second Ave. On the east corner (195 S. Juniper) is the Stafford Block of buildings. It is designed in the Streamline Moderne style with soaring towers and rounded forms. A style of the 1930s, World War II delayed the construction until 1948. A dry cleaners originally occupied the corner location.

Cross Juniper

249 E. Grand Ave. — This was the Piggly Wiggly Market. Built in 1931 it was enlarged in 1941. Later, a Rexall Drugs occupied the building for many years.

241 E. Grand Ave. — This distinctive entrance was built when it was the Carousel Children's Store, a children's clothing store.

237 E. Grand Ave. — The Times-Advocate newspaper office operated here from 1923 until 1953. It was the first building constructed to house Percy Evan's daily newspaper. Percy kept his desk in the window so he could keep an eye on the street and watch for news. He was also an Olivia Typewriter distributor. In 1953 the T-A, as it was known locally, moved to Ohio Street, which is now E. Valley Parkway.

Escondido City Hall and Escondido Mutual Water Co. – c. 1930

231 E. Grand Ave. — This is the location of Escondido's City Hall from 1892-1938. The building was remodeled in 1940 as a joint office of San Diego Water Co. and the Escondido Mutual Water Co.

215 E. Grand Ave. — From 1893-1923 Alvin Dunn published The Advocate, a weekly newspaper at this location in a wood framed building. The Advocate, which was agriculturally oriented, competed with The Times, which concentrated on the business community, for nearly two decades before the newspapers merged to become The Times-Advocate. After Dunn's wooden building was moved to S. Escondido Boulevard, a plaid brick store was built here in 1925. It was renovated in the late 1980s including facade restoration.

Interior of the Time-Advocate interior – 1914

The southeast corner of Kalmia has been the site of several different buildings. First it was the location of the Avenue House; it was a boarding house with a small dining room used by downtown merchants and others. It had a large garden with a fountain that was turned on during special occasions. The corner was later the site of the Pala Theatre and then a bowling alley.

Avenue House, a rooming house on Grand Ave. & Kalmia St. – c. 1890

Cross Kalmia

Look south on Kalmia, to the building just past the alley (122 S. Kalmia). Built in 1911, this was Louis Havens' original photography studio. Historians today are indebted to Havens for documenting Escondido, its people and events, from 1911 through 1944. A tall thin man with a large format camera, he was a common sight around town. He and his wife lived in an apartment above the studio.

Next door is 126 S. Kalmia. There are two iron horse rings in front of this building; it was the Palm Mortuary from 1932 to 1959.

On the Northeast corner of Kalmia and 2nd Ave is the Trenton Apartments at 204 E. 2nd. Contractor Samuel M. Stewart built Escondido's first apartment house in 1912 for Peter Schnack, an early Escondido photographer. Architecturally unique for Escondido and its time, the building has a placito (small plaza) in the center that can be viewed from all apartments on both floors. The placito was planted with semi-tropical plants, including banana trees. Originally called the Schnack Apartments, at the outbreak of the Great War (World War I) the name was changed to the Trenton Apartments due to anti-German sentiment. Schnack was from Trenton, New Jersey.

Now focus again on Grand Ave.

157 E. Grand Ave. — The Lyon family established a well beloved store, the Escondido Mercantile, in this corner building. The popular store later split into two stores, with The Mercantile carrying women's fashion and The Wardrobe, located further west on the block, for men's clothing. The building has been extensively remodeled.

155 E. Grand Ave. — At one time this was Escondido Hardware. This is also the location where Samuel Brannin died on the upper floor of an unknown business. Brannin was California's first millionaire, but was broke when he died here.

129 E. Grand Ave. — This building won a Governor's award for preservation. A general mercantile that was built here in 1907 burned after less than a year. During renovations during the 1980s burned timbers were found and the mural on the east wall was restored. The facade, while not original, is designed in the spirit of the original building.

As you approach the corner of Grand Ave. and Broadway St., and the tour's end, note buildings at 125 through 105 E. Grand Ave. They were originally two story brick buildings. Like other brick buildings on the street they were taken down to one story due to liability issues relating to earthquakes and un-reinforced brick.

From Grand Ave. go up Broadway St. three blocks,
to Pennsylvania Ave. and Grape Day Park.

Corner of Grand Ave. & Broadway – 1958

THE GRAPE DAY CELEBRATION
Grape Day Park

The annual Grape Day celebration has its roots in 1905, when long term water bond certificates were burned in front of the Lime Street School. Although the bonds had been paid off the previous year, California Admissions Day — September 9th of 1905 — had been selected for the event.

The Escondido event continued annually until 1908, when the name was changed to Grape Day, in support of the variety of grapes and wines which had made Escondido famous. The field behind the school had been the site of many previous community celebrations, and the Grape Day event continued to be held there.

Festival promoters invited southern California to view and sample the wide variety of Escondido produce, and the parade and fair were perhaps the second most popular in the state, only to the Rose Parade, held in Pasadena. Over 1,000 people attended that first year.

The Grape Day festival was developed to promote the grape harvest, and thousands of pounds of grapes were given away. The event also was held to boost the agriculture of the

Grape Day float – 1910

community, and visitors from all over San Diego county came to the fair in Escondido.

Originally arriving by train, thousands of people came to enjoy the festivities and see the harvest. The parade began at the train station and came up Grand Avenue, with the street decorated and lined with booths, showing off the produce, farm animals, and of course grapes. Each year, the parade ended at Grape Day Park, where awards were given for the best in agricultural crops and animals.

Escondido Creek flows adjacent to the old school grounds and floods in 1909, weakened the building structure. The Lime Street School was torn down in and in 1910, the school grounds became officially, Grape Day Park. The following year, the Chamber of Commerce bought the land and landscaped the park just for Grape Day.

Train passengers arriving at the Depot for Grape Day – 1908

Today, the two palm trees that were in front of the Lime Street School, stand in memory of the little school that had stood there since 1887. Pepper trees also continue to grow from those early days and the large eucalyptus was once three trees from that time, now grown together.

People arriving for Grape Day – 1913

Grape Day Float – 1919

Grape Day Quee, Agnes Ayers – 1923

178 pound bunch of grapes – Grape Day 1925

Grape Day booths – Grand Ave. – 1908

*Gas filled balloon above the Grape Day activities –
1908*

Queens Float in the Grape Day parade – 1926

THE ESCONDIDO HISTORY CENTER
Grape Day Park

Housed within Grape Day Park is the Escondido History Center. The Escondido Library building of 1895, was moved into Grape Day park in 1971. The realignment of Grand Avenue east, had caused its removal, and this became the first historical building in the celebrated park. Designated an American Bicentennial project, the Library was renovated and opened in 1976 as the office of the Escondido Historical Society. It was the City's 88th anniversary; a time capsule buried in the park is to be opened in 2076.

The Library opened as a museum in 1976.

A Native American grinding rock (Indian metate,) was donated to the Historical Society in 1977 and the ten ton rock was moved there by crane in October of that year.

The Victorian Country Home, built in 1890, was moved to Grape Day Park in 1980. Renovated by Historical Society members, the home opened for viewing in 1986. The Queen Anne

Victorian Country Home.

farmhouse is a redwood structure of eight rooms and has seven gables. It is covered in both shingle and shiplap siding and is about 1700 square feet in size. The adjacent tank house was rebuilt in 2004 and a 1920s metal windmill stands behind. Water pumped up into the tank and was then gravity fed to the farmhouse.

The Penner Barn dates from 1901, and was rebuilt by the Kiwanis Club in 1976 by using the original siding around a newly constructed frame.

The Penner Barn

The barn contains agricultural equipment relating to Escondido's grape and citrus industries. The windmill in front of the barn, dates from the early 20th century. It actually came to Escondido from Nebraska in 1970, and was later moved to the park in 1999. The Dempster windmill (Vaneless #3), is a constant velocity windmill, tilting the vanes automatically as the wind speed changes. It was restored by the Historical Society over several years.

The Blacksmith shop is a replica built in 1993 of the 1908 Bandy Blacksmith shop. The blacksmith equipment is from the old Bandy shop, on North Kalmia. Blacksmithing is still taught in the building which houses the Ari de Jong Teaching Facility. The Bandy outhouse was brought to the park in 1993.

The Bandy Blacksmiths Shop

Along with the beginnings of the City of Escondido, the Santa Fe Depot was constructed in 1888. After WWII, passenger trains stopped coming, and the depot closed in 1978. The Historical Society ran the Save Our Local Depot campaign and moved the station to the park in 1984. The depot is of Victorian Stick-Style architecture, with both fishscale shingle and shiplap siding, along with horizontal and vertical stickwork. The depot contains historical exhibits, railway furniture, and photographs.

The Santa Fe Depot.

The Pullman Railroad Car #92, is a rare example of a passenger and postal railway car. Restored, it contains a mailroom and passenger area. Also inside the railway car is a HO Scale model railroad, that shows the 22 mile run from Oceanside to Escondido.

Pullman Railroad Car #92

Grape Day Park now contains Vinehenge, a large playground and public art project. Dedicated during the Grape Day festivities in 2004, Vinehenge features vine climbing equipment, grape leaf seats, and a large grape slide.

Vinehenge – playground – 2005

★ Escondido History ★

APPENDICES

Historic Home Walking Tour

Street names

Bibliography

Photo Album

Index

Colophon

★ Escondido History ★

Historic Home Walking Tour

The city's first neighborhood is now the Old Escondido Historic District. Its boundaries are Escondido Blvd to the west, 5th Avenue to the north, Chestnut to the east and 13th to the south. During Escondido's early years, nearly everything beyond this neighborhood was undeveloped or in agriculture.

The area became a historic district in 1992. Neighbors working together to preserve the historic character of their unique neighborhood formed a non-profit group that actively works to improve the Historic District. A handful of historic homes are open to the public each year at their popular Mother's Day Home Tour, their primary fundraiser. The Old Escondido neighborhood has a mix of 19th century Victorians, early 20th century bungalows and mid-century homes.

Start at the northeast corner of Broadway and 5th Avenue for a walking tour of the Historic District. Today's numbered streets (running east to west) were originally named for states. The street names were changed in 1930 when the post office started home mail delivery. While standing at the corner, look down to notice street names incised in the sidewalk. On this particular corner, both names are wrong since Broadway was originally Lime Street and this section of 5th Ave was Dakota. Watch for street names incised on corners throughout the historic district.

Homes on this walking tour are, for the most part, some of the earliest homes built in Escondido. As you walk through the Historic District make sure to note and appreciate the many wonderful homes built later. There are many bungalows built in the first several decades of the 20th century in the neighborhood. Contact the Escondido History Center to take a guided walking tour that includes information about more historic homes than those listed here.

Go east on 5th and watch for the following homes, which will be on both sides of the street. Remember that these are private residences and are NOT open to the public. Please respect their occupants' privacy.

128 E. 5th - This house was built for Ed Hatch circa 1890, probably by architect Jesse Pomeroy. Hatch moved to Escondido in 1886; he was a painter and then a rancher. Later he became the manager for Escondido's first telephone exchange. Other positions he held include Wells Fargo agent, bakery owner, and Justice of the Peace.

143 E. 5th - Alvin D. Dunn was the first owner of this 1906 house. He was the owner and founder of the local newspaper The Advocate. Like many homes, this house has architectural elements representing more than one style: in this case California Four-square, Classical Revival and Queen Anne. This home represents a more simple version of Victorian architecture, which is often elaborate. The small second floor balcony is a later addition.

208 E. 5th Avenue - This National Register property is an 1886 Victorian with a 1908 Classical Revival addition on the east side. It was built of redwood for George V. Thomas. His four brothers were founders of the Escondido Land & Town Company. Although not

The George Thomas house on 5th Ave. at Kalmia St.

officially a member of the EL&TCo., George came to Escondido at their request to run a lumber company that supplied the young community with building materials. His daughter married a Turrentine, another prominent Escondido family whose members included judges, mayors and business owners. It is one of the oldest buildings in the city and the only home of its era to remain in the same family. It is currently occupied by the 4th generation of the same Thomas-Turrentine family.

On the northern corners of 5th at Ivy you'll notice another set of incised street names that are both outdated. The street names listed are Curve Street and 7th Ave. Curve was named because the street curves around the base of the old "high school hill." Part of the old Curve Street is Ivy, and the rest is 2nd Ave today. Escondido's original numbered streets were between Juniper and Ash and numbered 1st through 8th. Grand Avenue originally ended at the hotel (today's Palomar Medical Center) and then curved around it to the north. After Grand was extended to go straight through, what had been 3rd became Grand Ave. 1st became Pennsylvania and 2nd became Ohio. The old 4th through 8th Avenues are today 2nd through 6th.

408, 418, 424, and 438 E. 5th - In this row of Craftsman houses each has unique Craftsman elements. 408 has an unusually wide roof overhang and gables face each direction. 418 has a gable porch roof with a small hip, and dentil trim along the entire front fascia board. 424's graceful eyebrow porch roof is supported by round columns on square piers. 438 has a high foundation that gives it added height, the gabled dormers and deep porch makes this house feel substantial.

455 E. 5th Ave - John Lloyd Wright, the 19-year-old draftsman son of Frank Lloyd Wright designed this 1913 Prairie-School house. It was Wright's first house project and was based on his famous father's Ladies Home Journal house of 1906. It was also contractor W.W. Beckler's first project. The home cost $3,200 plus a 10% architectural fee. Note the deep overhang, band of

windows, and large bay windows.

Turn right on Hickory and then right on 6th Ave.

444 6th - Probably designed by Jesse Pomeroy who designed the house at the Escondido History Center in Grape Day Park and the Hatch House on 5th. The unusual inset dormers were a trademark of his. It was built circa 1895.

421, 415 and 307 E. 6th - This trio of Queen Anne cottages were built circa 1889. Different details on each home distinguish the similar overall design. 309 was originally located on Juniper at the corner of 6th, but was moved around the corner to this location.

Turn left onto Juniper.

537 S. Juniper - On the northwest corner of 6th and Juniper is a craftsman bungalow, built circa 1914. Note the separate roof and gable for the porch and gracefully tapered door trim. It was the home of Dr. David Crise, one of Escondido's early physicians. His

Brewer family backyard, 831 E. 3rd Ave. – c. 1930

son Bruce was also a doctor and went into practice with his father. David also served on Escondido's Board of Education around the turn of the 20th century.

604 S. Juniper - On the southeast corner at 6th is a Mediterranean Revival house built in 1915 and noted for its fine details. The flat roof has a wide tile-covered cornice slanting around the entire perimeter and covering the porte-cochere.

Grandma Stiles in front of her home on W. Grand Ave. – 1896

638 S. Juniper - Julius H. Anderson, cashier of the Bank of Escondido, bought this lot for $325.00 and built a Queen Anne house. It is likely that the architectural firm of Comstock and Trotsche designed the building. They designed the Bank of Escondido and the San Diego residence of the Timken family that the third floor of this home strongly resembles. Later owners included Escondido Times business manager N. Frederick Hansen, former Iowa State Senator

Abraham O. Garlock, blacksmith Tom Bandy and 1980s City Councilman Ed Struiksma.

700 S. Juniper - The Beach house is the most elaborate Victorian home in the city. The 1896 Queen Anne Victorian is a National Register property. It was built by real estate broker and insurance agent Albert H. Beach, who owned one of the first businesses in the city. Later, Amelia, daughter of roller-bearing king Henry H. Timken, and her husband Appleton Bridges lived in the home for a short time. The home's circular porch faces the corner and has a six-sided bay window. This large home underwent a meticulous renovation in the late 1990s.

637 S. Juniper - Built around the time of incorporation, the building material makes this home noteworthy. This small Italianate house was built of Escondido brick. A brickyard was established in the city in 1886 to supply the treeless city with building materials. This may have been built as a spec house by the Escondido Land & Town

Thomas' Model House – 1889

Company, like their Model House located at 969 West 3rd. Most bricks produced locally were used to build commercial buildings in the young community. The first of several wooden additions was built in 1908 and included the porch.

801 S. Juniper - Two things make this house stand out: the attention to detail and its very unusual history. Bob Beacon began construction on the house in 1923. He was a socially prominent eccentric who was gifted in design and building. Skilled craftsman built the home using the finest woods and materials. The elaborate interior was exquisitely crafted. Beacon worked on the house for 10 years but never finished it and never lived in it. Then he left town for over twenty years, leaving the house unfinished. It became known as "the ghost house of Escondido" and also "Beacon's Folly." As a child, Mary Wagor played in and around the boarded up house. Decades later when Beacon returned to Escondido Mary persuaded her husband Dick Einer purchased the home. In the basement garage the Einers found a Pierce-Arrow in almost perfect condition. They finished the house, moved in and lived here for decades. Note the log trim facing the double gables, carved wood trim over the recessed entry and the two narrow bay windows.

1006 S. Juniper Street - This imposing home is one of the city's showcases. Built it 1887, it is an Italianate Victorian whose original brick has been stuccoed. A kitchen has been added to the rear, and a carriage house on the north side. Valentine Katzenberger, a plasterer and bricklayer, built this imposing home. He also built the Bank of Escondido on Grand at Lime and the Model House at 969 W. 3rd. The year after the house was built the Escondido Land & Town Company sold the home to the builder's parents, Franz and Elizabeth Katzenberger. In 1905 Lewis B. Hooper purchased the property. It was a 10 acre tract that went from 8th to 13th Ave. Hooper built a tennis court just south of the house and their driveway eventually became 10th Ave. A farmer when he came to Escondido, Hooper got into real estate a few years later and was City Treasurer in 1911. He donated property on Kalmia at 3rd to the city for the Carnegie Library, which was built in 1910.

Go west on 10th Ave.

146 W. 10th Ave - This large Tudor-style Craftsman house is on a double lot. A very high gable roof covers the two story house. It was built in 1910 for Fred and Helen Hall. Fred was vice-president of First National Bank at Grand and Lime. The Halls entertained on a grand scale in the 3 story home until Fred Hall was murdered (at another property) when a disgruntled customer mistook him for another bank employee. Later owners include Frank B and Delia Hunt who owned Escondido Hardware and Furniture, grocery store owner Jesse O. Shelby, Ford dealer Homer Heller and his wife Helen, and Superintendent of the high school district Dr. John Cooper.

Martin Ranch looking NW / Citrus & Glenridge Rd. – 1923

203 W. 10th Ave - This one-story Craftsman bungalow is probably unique in the city. The very unusual flagstone cladding and Spanish tile roof sets this house apart. Built circa 1920, it has a conventional floor plan.

Go north on Maple.

832 Maple Street - Sitting high above the street on nearly a half acre is a Queen Ann cottage. The home was built circa 1892, but look for a marking of "1913" on the perimeter wall.

204 W. 8th - On the northwest corner of Maple and 8th is the Culp house. It was built circa 1890. Brothers Reuben, Luther and Morris Culp arrived in Escondido that year 1890 and found ready employment as carpenters. Luther Culp built this modest Queen Anne farmhouse with wraparound porch. He later became superintendent of streets, city marshal, and tax collector.

Continue north on Maple and then turn left on 7th.

208 W. 7th - This fine Craftsman home was built in 1911. A heavy roof and full-length porch with tapered columns add to the solid feeling of this home.

Escondido Cornet Band

Go east on 7th.

109 W. 7th - Escondido's first barber, Leo Escher, built this house in 1887. Escher was also drum major for the city's band. The Queen Anne Victorian has been expanded over the years, with a two-story addition on the west side. The house originally occupied the entire corner and had a large cistern behind the house.

710 S. Broadway - On the southeast corner of Broadway and 7th is the Hick House. It faces 7th but has a Broadway address. One of the city's earliest homes, construction started in late 1886 and the home was occupied in early 1887. Richard S. and Emeline Hick built the home. R. S. Hick was a lawyer, and Kansas senator. As a lawyer during Escondido's formative years, he drew up many of the city's ordinances. One ordinance he wrote made Escondido a dry town, even though the first crop heavily promoted in the young city was grapes. It read, "Forfeiture of title if intoxicating liquors are manufactured or disposed of on said land" and was on all parcel titles. He was often referred to as Judge Hick, but that may have been an honorary title. In 1890 the family returned to Kansas. Extensively changed over the years when it was divided into apartments, a massive restoration returned it to a single family home.

Head toward to your starting point on 5th.

You will approach Central School, the oldest school operating in Escondido. Parts of the current school were built in 1938.

Originally this was the site of the 5th Avenue School. The two-story brick building opened in 1910. In the 1920s the school expanded across Maple and took up both blocks between Broadway and Escondido Blvd. The original brick building on the 100 block was torn down as a result of the Field Act, which passed after the devastating 1933 Long Beach earthquake, and was responsible for the destruction of hundreds of schools state-wide.

Eventually the school shrunk back down to just this block.

The school name was changed to Central School in 1942. In 1951 the school divided when Central Middle School split off.

Central School – 5th Ave. and Maple St. – 1948

ESCONDIDO ROADS

The roads in town for Escondido, orginate from the 1886 survey. Grand Avenue and Lime Street (Broadway) have always been the center of town for Escondido. *Avenues* were named for U.S. States and ran east and west, while *Streets* were named for mostly agricultural trees and ran north and south. North. of Pennsylvania, *Avenues* were later named for presidents.

State names were changed in 1930 to numbered streets, when the U.S. Post Office, began home delivery. Some state names are still preserved as imprints in a few sidewalks.

STREETS	TODAY	NOTE
Ash		
Beech		
Cedar		
Date		
Elm		
Fig		
Grape		
Hickory		
Ivy	2nd	Ivy south (& 2nd east)
Juniper		
Kalmia		
Lime	Broadway (1930)	
Maple		
Nutmeg	Escondido Blvd.	(also was San Diego)
Orange		
Pine	Centre City	
Quince		
Redwood		
Spruce		
Tulip		
Upas		
Vine		

AVENUES	TODAY	NOTE
Lincoln		
Grant	Mission	
Washington		
Pennsylvania		(1st 1930)
Ohio	Valley Parkway	(2nd east of Hickory)
Grand		(3rd east of Hickory)
Indiana	2nd (1930)	(4th east of Hickory)
Iowa	3rd (1930)	(5th east of Hickory)
Illinois	4th (1930)	(6th east of Hickory)
Dakota	5th (1930)	(7th east of Hickory)
Nebraska	6th (1930)	(8th east of Hickory)
Minnesota	7th (1930)	
Delaware	8th (1930)	
Kansas	9th (1930)	
Nevada	10th (1930)	
Georgia	11th (1930)	
Maine	12th (1930)	
Florida	13th (1930)	
Idaho	15th (1930)	

BIBLIOGRAPHY

Lorey, Frank III; The Gold Mining Days of Escondido; Escondido Historical Society, Escondido CA, 2000

Buskirk, Nick & Shirley; Escondido Union High School District; Heritage Publishing Co., Encinitas CA, 1994

Buskirk, Nick & Shirley; Escondido Then and Now; Heritage Publishing Co., Encinitas CA, 1993

McGrew, Alan B.; Hidden Valley Heritage; Blue-Ribbon Centennial History Committee, Escondido CA, 1988

Ryan, Francis B. & Lewis C.; Mini-Guide to Historic Escondido; Self Published, Escondido CA, 1984

Ryan, Francis B. & Lewis C.; Escondido, As It Was; Self Published, Escondido CA, 1980

Escondido Historical Society; Escondido, A Pictorial History; Self Published, Escondido CA, 1982

Ryan, Francis B. & Lewis C.; Yesterdays in Escondido; Self Published, Escondido CA, 1973

Ryan, Francis B. & Lewis C.; Early Days in Escondido; Self Published, Escondido CA, 1970

Roberts, Elizabeth Judson; Indian Stories of the South West; Harr Wagner Publishing Co., San Francisco CA, 1917

Northrop, Marie; Spanish ~ Mexican Families of Early California Vol I; Southern California Genealogical Society, Burbank CA 1986/1999

Northrop, Marie; Spanish ~ Mexican Families of Early California Vol II; Southern California Genealogical Society, Burbank CA 1984/1999

Northrop, Marie; Spanish ~ Mexican Families of Early California Vol III; Southern California Genealogical Society, Burbank CA 2005

Robinson, W. W.; Land in California; University of California Press, Berkeley CA, 1948/1979

Gudde, Erwin G.; California Place Names; University of California Press, Berkeley CA, 1949/1974

Beck, Warren A. & Haase, Ynez D.; Historical Atlas of California; University of Oklahoma Press, Norman OK, 1974

Oakeshott, Gordon B.; California's Changing Landscapes; McGraw-Hill Book Co. New York NY, 1971

Photo Album

Escondido High School – 1895

Chicago Millinery Store on Grand Ave. – 1895

Inside Butler Barber Shop – 100 E. Grand Ave. – 1914

Inside the citrus packing house – c. 1909

1918 Escondido Stage – 100 block of E. Grand Ave.

Lobby of the Charlotta Hotel – 637 S. Upas – c. 1920

Marshall Luther Culp – town marshall 1910-1916

SE view of Grand Ave. & Broadway – 1909

Grape Day – giving away 10 tons of grapes – Grape Day Park, 1913

Grape Day horse group – 1911

Grape Day crowd in the park – 1912

Hydroplane at Grape Day – 1918

Red Crown Gasoline Station

View of Grand Ave. at Broadway looking east – 1951

Escondido Lemon Assoc – 222 N. Tulip St. – c. 1945

Escondido Orange Assoc –1155 W. Mission Ave.– 1950

Grand Ave. & Broadway NW corner – c. 1935

Palomar Hospital – 550 E. Grand Ave. – 1950

Grape Day tractor co. display – 1949

Escondido High School Gymnasium

INDEX

A

B

C

★ Index ★

Y

COLOPHON

This book is set in Caxton, a *Garalde* typeface. Designed by Leslie Usherwood in 1981 for Letraset, it is of an old style design, with a large x-height (small letters.) Having short serifs and high-waisted capitals, it is a text face intended for use in journals and books. The design makes it easy to read in small point sizes.

The typestyle is named for William Caxton, an early printer and the first person to publish in English during 1471, while he was in the Netherlands. He is primarily known for publishing Chaucer's Canterbury Tales in England.